THE LOOP APPROACH

Sebastian Klein is a psychologist and organizational coach. He has worked in management consulting and has co-founded several startups in the media field. Currently, he's a partner at the transformation consultancy TheDive, which helps organizations of all sizes explore new ways of collaboration.

Ben Hughes heads the content team at Blinkist. A Berlin-based company, Blinkist inspires millions of people to keep learning by offering key insights from nonfiction books. Ben is also a former management consultant, current mindfulness enthusiast and author of two books of science experiments for children.

The LOOP Approach

Campus Verlag
Frankfurt / New York

The original edition was published in 2019 by Campus Verlag with the titel *Der Loop-Approach. Wie Du Deine Organisation von innen heraus transformierst.* All rights reserved.

ISBN 978-3-593-51120-7   Print
ISBN 978-3-593-44245-7   E-Book (PDF)
ISBN 978-3-593-44244-0   E-Book (EPUB)

Cover design: total italic, Thierry Wijnberg, Amsterdam/Berlin and Studio Dominik Wagner
Typesetting: Fotosatz L. Huhn, Linsengericht
Fonts: Roboto and Skolar
Printing: Beltz Grafische Betriebe GmbH, Bad Langensalza
Printed in Germany

www.campus.de

CONTRIBUTORS

The Loop Approach was developed at TheDive, and was only made possible by the contributions of Hie-suk Yang, Frederik Fleischmann, Jörn Apel, Marianne Skvorc, Uli Schoop, Eva Hohenberger, Simon Berkler, Maya Biersack, Simon Hofer, Lena Marbacher, Dominik Wagner, Georg Tarne, Eduard Munkhart, and Jaqueline Stein. The approach was further developed and tested together with countless great people at our partner companies, like Audi Business Innovation, Deutsche Bahn, Deutsche Telekom, and Europace.

Special thanks to Anja Michalski, Martin Wiens, Lena Marbacher, Dominik Wagner, Robert Lösel, Louka Goetzke, and Eva Hohenberger who also played an active part in the creation of this book.

The authors Sebastian Klein and Ben Hughes first began contemplating the future of work while working together at the start-up Blinkist. Many thanks to the people there who were part of and made possible this first part of the journey.

This book also draws inspiration and ideas from the world-wide community of Holacracy practitioners, as well as Nonviolent Communication enthusiasts in Germany and the rest of Europe.

It's been a fascinating, thrilling ride, and we look forward to what's next!

YOU ARE
HERE

PART 2

The LOOP

THE

The 7 Habits of
Highly Effective
Organizations

MODULE 1
Clarity

Approach

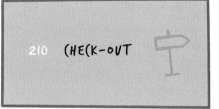

PART 3
ARRIVAL

PART 1

LAUNCH

Let's start with a check-in.

Whenever we want to do something well, we always start our work with a check-in. Checking in is the simple act of stepping back, taking a deep breath, and affirming to others that we're really there, present in the moment. Making time for this short break helps us understand our own intentions and communicate them to others, thereby getting everyone on the same page. If someone's mind is still dwelling on last night's Margarita Monday or on their life crisis, they shed such preoccupations here.

Typically, a check-in takes the form of two simple questions, which everyone present answers in turn. So to get you started on your journey of working through this book together with us, please answer the following questions.

What's on your mind?
What has your attention right now?

Take as much time as you need.

Just like you, we find ourselves taking part in a major transformation that's gripping the world right now. A transformation that's fundamentally changing the way people work together in organizations. The rigid hierarchies of old are being replaced by new, more flexible organizational models, and this will be arguably the greatest organizational upheaval since the Industrial Revolution.

And as with most revolutions, there's just no ignoring this one. New organizational models will become the status quo, and traditional hierarchies will fall along the wayside of history, like steam engines and fax machines before them. We can't imagine going back to a world without electricity, airplanes or the internet, and soon, the same will be true of these new organizational models.

But why is this revolution happening? If you've ever worked in a corporation that's organized as a traditional hierarchy, you probably also recognize and appreciate that change is sorely needed. Until recently, it was commonly accepted that if you wanted to get any larger group of people to work together, the *pyramid*[1] model was the only way to go. But today, it is becoming increasingly obvious that the era of the pyramid is over. And while there are many reasons for this, we want to highlight three:

First, people find it very demotivating to work in a rigid hierarchy, where they're just expected to do as they're told. Young, well-educated professionals entering the workforce today are no longer willing to sacrifice years of their career to just following orders from pointy-haired bosses. After all, they can afford to be picky: the market for good talent is competitive, meaning employees are no longer desperate to cling on to whatever stable job they can. The most sought-after professionals demand much more than a steady paycheck: they want meaning, flexibility, and to be trusted with the authority to make decisions that actually impact the organization.

---

1   We use the term "pyramid" as a simplified term for the structure of a traditional management hierarchy.

Second, the rigid, hierarchical pyramids of the past are just too slow and cumbersome to succeed in competition with young, agile upstarts. Without the burden of a pyramid on their shoulders, the newcomers are much faster at adapting to their changing environment. As a result, they are inventing and reinventing businesses faster than the old guard can even fathom, let alone compete with. If established corporations used to laugh off small startups operating from garages somewhere, their smirks have since been thoroughly wiped off their faces. As companies like Amazon, Facebook and Google have proved, any scrappy newcomer could skyrocket to the top of the Fortune 500 list in under a decade, leaving former industry leaders in the dust. The age of the dinosaurs is over—the mammals are here, baby!

Third, if we take a big picture view, we rapidly see that our world desperately needs new kinds of organizations. From accelerating climate change to increasing inequality, we believe that many of humanity's biggest challenges today stem from our sadly out-of-date organizational model. Countless organizations emerging today have already adopted the greater purpose of changing the world for the better, and they only continue to evolve around this purpose[2]. Many such companies have already entered the spotlight via Frederic Laloux's book *Reinventing Organizations*. And in our own work, we see more new purpose-driven companies similar to Patagonia, Burtzoorg, and Zappos emerging every week. What's more, we're also excited to see many larger organizations—or at least parts of them—take on the challenge of reinventing themselves and boldly reorganizing how people work within them.

---

[2] Please note, though, that adopting a new organizational model and wielding a positive impact on the world don't always go hand in hand. Just consider companies like Amazon or Facebook—hardly prime examples of new organizations using their power for good. But they do demonstrate nicely just how effective the new organizational models can be.

A new mindset

What we're currently witnessing in the world around us is a great shift from one dominant type of organizational operating system[3] to another. The old, hierarchical management pyramid, which for millenia seemed like the only viable option for running any larger organization, is finally being replaced by more network-like models. But this "update" isn't going smoothly. Not at all. In fact, it's generating lots of tension and friction.

On the one hand, we have a new generation of companies that's instinctively embracing new way of doing things. They adopt ready-made solutions like Holacracy, or design their own, and just go with it. Meanwhile, most companies still run on the old operating system, and for them, updating to a new one is no easy task (yes, even worse than Windows 10). Though the software analogy can make it sound like companies just need to press a button to update and reboot, the truth is that it's much more complicated and arduous. And the older and larger an organization, the harder and more painful the transformation will be.

So does this mean that all the old "tankers" weighed down by pyramids are doomed to rust in their old docks and sink? Or can they be refitted with the new operating system, making them agile and nimble skiffs once again? These aren't easy questions to answer. But one thing we know for sure: it's not

---

3   We'll explain this term in more detail in the glossary at the end of this book. For now, it's enough to understand that it encompasses all the ground rules an organization has defined for itself, such as its decision processes, leadership guidelines and meeting protocols.

enough to just put a fresh coat of paint on a rusted structure. What's needed is a fundamental shift of mindset within the organization.

The classical management hierarchy operated under a mindset of "predict and control," with those at the top of the pyramid making plans and commanding those below to execute. But today, this mindset is being unseated by one called "sense and respond." Instead of a few clever brains deciding what should be done, the power to "sense" new information and make decisions as to how to respond is distributed throughout the organization. This means that every member of a company becomes an intelligent sensor, receiving and evaluating signals from the outside world and then responding to them autonomously, without asking their bosses for approval.

The upshot?

Rather than waiting around for information and decisions to percolate up and down a hierarchy, an organization can make thousands of smart decisions every hour. Even better, they are made by the true experts on the ground, not the suit bossing them around thanks to a degree in executive hand-shaking.

But how are these large organizations, which have basically ruled the world until now, supposed to "change their mindset"? With hundreds or even thousands of employees, what should they do and where should they start?

Failures and success stories

It's no wonder that the prospect of this shift is already leading to great uncertainty or even panic within some organizations. And this isn't helped by the constant articles, case-studies and keynote presentations recounting cautionary tales of transformations gone wrong. For instance, stories of some organizations trying to become more agile and self-organized but only ending up more chaotic as a result. Or how others got off to a promising start and scored some initial wins in the transformation, but then quickly ran into huge obstacles that no-one foresaw.

But these tales are only disheartening if viewed through a certain lens, namely the assumption that we ought already to know exactly what the organization of the future should look like. Putting aside this assumption, the stories become something else: chronicles of brave people venturing out into the great unknown. We cannot expect perfection from explorers setting sail on an uncharted ocean: under such wild uncertainty, just discovering the first few islands should be considered a major success. It's easy to forget that even Columbus technically failed at what he set out to do: finding a shortcut to Asia.

One such success story, to our mind at least, is that of Zappos, the American online shoeretailer founded in 1999. In 2013, the company introduced Holacracy[4] as its official operating system, and things started out swimmingly. Many people applauded as Zappos made the bold move to get rid of its managers.

But as is often the case with change, this initial success was followed by a swathe of new challenges. It rapidly became clear just how difficult it is to transform a 1,500-strong organization. The shift required everyone to throw many old behaviors overboard, and no-one likes doing that.

For Zappos, the process turned out to be time-consuming, non-linear and controversial. Many employees were unhappy about the move and left the company. Eventually, Zappos even had to step back from a comprehensive implementation of Holacracy. And now, over five years since the transformation started, it is still far from complete.

---

4   In the next part of this book you'll find a short explanation on what Holacracy is. For now, it's enough to know that it's one of the operating systems that companies can use to organize people within them. You could call it software for people that aims to replace the old power structures in organizations.

Into uncharted waters

Of course, the story of Zappos can easily be seen as a cautionary tale. If you wanted to, you could use it to bolster a case that any organizational operating system beyond the classical hierarchy simply won't work in the real world. But to do so would be to take an overly simplistic view of how transformations in complex systems work.

That's because complex systems can't be transformed just by opening a can of ready-made solution and painting over the old one. The very notion that this is possible is a fallacy baked into the old predict-and-control mindset, which is obsessed with top-down solutions. But as we can see from the example of Zappos, a successful transformation requires a new mindset. And we believe this mindset is "sense and respond."

Here, the transformation is a never-ending process, marked by learning along the way, casting old assumptions overboard and always looking for the sensible next step to take. Of course, this approach isn't easy; it requires a lot of work and constant rethinking. But we're convinced it's worth it.

Our model, The Loop Approach, is intended to help you start such a transformation journey and navigate it safely. This book is by no means a one-size-fits-all blueprint for a successful transformation, but it will hopefully help you plan and guide one. It does so by providing a structure for something that we've found is intrinsically hard to plan, while still leaving room to maneuver around individual circumstances. It comprises a process, but still remains open and flexible enough to be adapted to each organization's needs and constraints.

Why this book?

Over the past few years, we've spent a lot of time reading and thinking about the future of work and how to get there. We've tried various approaches ourselves and worked with many clients and partners trying to answer the question: How can we transform an existing system without breaking it?

The answer is that the process is invariably complex and non-linear, which makes it very challenging for most organizations operating under the old predict-and-control mindset to pursue. Meanwhile, consultants and coaches are excitedly screaming dozens of new buzzwords at them, adding to the sense of overwhelm and leaving these organizations wondering about things like:

"What does agile have to do with self-organization? Do we all need to be ambidextrous now? Do our employees need to become design thinkers? When and where are new systems like Holacracy helpful, and where do they just complicate things?"

The usual change process

Destroy the old structure   The journey is undefined   Goal: We are agile now

Over the course of this book, we'll present our approach, which was developed to make transformations of all sizes manageable without stress-eating, hair-pulling, or fist-on-desk-pounding. We'll teach you the tools and behaviors that can best support a transformation toward an evolutionary, agile organization. And if you're skeptical about what exactly this transformation is supposed to look like, considering that it's based on the rather vague demand to "adopt a new mindset," fear not—we'll show you that too.

The Loop-Approach

Preserve the old structure   The journey is the destination   The end result is undefined

Can't we just decide on a name for next-level organizations already?

If you have any knowledge of the field of organizational development, you might already be wondering what we think the **correct** term for the organization of the future is. There are so many flying around already! Is it "teal", as Frederic Laloux says in *Reinventing Organizations*? Is it "evolutionary," as Aaron Dignan says in *Brave New Work*? Or maybe it's "agile," "self-organized," "next-level" or "Alice in Wonderland"? Our advice: relax. The label isn't the important part here, and in fact trying to pin down the "correct" one is pretty typical "predict-and-control" thinking. Our Loop Approach is all about the process, not the end result, because the result will be different for every transformation. So please feel free to call your organization whatever feels right. Call it fabulous for all we care! In this book, we'll use changing labels, but as you'll soon learn, for us they all mean pretty much the same thing.

In our experience, organizations spend far too much time trying to define the *What* (meaning the desired end result), when they should really be focusing on the *How* (the process of getting there). That's why one of our main goals in this book is to give you a set of useful tools for mapping out the *How*.

Before we start

Everybody makes mistakes. But with this book, we want to give you the tools to hopefully avoid the mistakes that others (including ourselves) have already made. What's more, we also want to encourage you to continue along this path you've chosen. The world needs brave pioneers like yourself, and organizations can only be transformed from within.

The Loop Approach has been developed to help you on this journey, whether you're just getting started or alread knee-deep in a transformation. Armed with it, you'll be better prepared to master the transformation process you're about to embark on, or to regain a firmer grasp of the one you perhaps find yourself in the midst of. But whatever you do, please don't consider this book complete. We certainly don't, and we plan to continue developing these tools further. Take the parts that you find useful, adapt them as you see fit, and then implement them out there in the roiling seas of real organizations. Meanwhile, if something seems useless or doesn't fit your organization, then please, go ahead and ignore it. And of course, if you feel something is missing or have any ideas for how we could make the Loop Approach even more useful for other pioneers, drop us a line! Just as we hope that you'll benefit from our experiences, future readers might benefit from yours. By sharing and learning, we can all nudge this necessary revolution forward one step at a time.

Last but not least, we have one more question for you. Whenever we start working on something, we ask each other: *what do you need?* This helps us align on our expectations. What's more, it also makes it easier to tell when we're actually done with our work, because we'll have defined what "done" means for each of us. Hence, we'd like to ask you: *What do you need? What are the big questions you're hoping to be able to answer by reading this book? What do you need to get out of it in order to say that choosing to read it was a worthwhile decision?* Jot down your answers somewhere, perhaps in the margins of this page like some Renaissance genius, or in the box provided like a regular person. Then, when you get to the end of the book, you can come back here to check if you got what you wanted.

What are the big questions you're hoping to be able to answer by reading this book?

What do you need to get out of it in order to say that choosing to read it was a successful decision?

THE PYRAMID

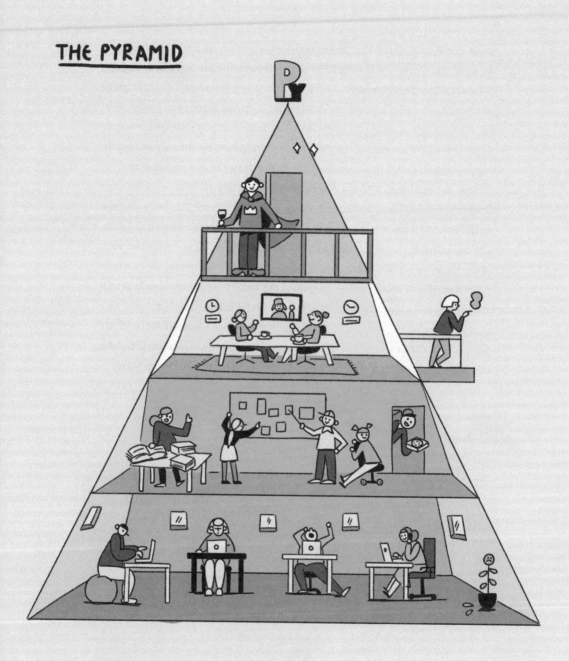

J ust a few decades ago, the world of organizations was much more straightforward than today. That's because it was generally acknowledged that the only right way to structure any large grouping of people was as a *pyramid*. In this rigidly hierarchical construction, all major decisions are taken by those at the top, and they pass down orders through the pyramid to the workers, employees, and minions on the lower levels, where the actual operative work takes place.

And looking at the arc of human history, we can see countless examples of how successful the pyramid model has been. One of the most massive and famous organizations run this way was the Roman empire, where the Emperor reigned supreme at the very top of the pyramid. From there, he used a vast machine of government and military officials to implement his commands. As a result, the Roman empire ruled over large parts of the world and shaped their development in ways that are still felt to this day.

With such compelling success stories to its name, it's no wonder that the pyramid has been the almost inevitable organizing principle for any operation involving more than a handful of people. From clans to villages, towns to cities, kingdoms to armies, countries to corporations, and coal mines to car factories, the pyramid was the way to go.

That's because the classical hierarchy of a pyramid is quite effective at reducing complexity in a system. It does this by creating clarity. Everyone knows exactly what he or she is supposed to do: just follow the orders given from above. What's more, large projects can be easily split up and shared among different parts of the organization, so the pyramid also works at scale.

COMMAND & CONTROL

But, you may now be thinking, if the pyramid model is so fine and dandy, then why did we say before that change is sorely needed?

Tankers cannot navigate these stormy times

Just a few decades ago, most organizations found themselves operating in relatively stable environments. Sure, there were plenty of revolutionary technological developments and political upheavals before the late 20th century too, but in general, these were rare and unfolded more slowly than today. In an environment that didn't change much year to year, companies could also expect the same business model to work for decades, with at most only minor tinkering needed to keep them competitive. And the pyramid is a great organizational model for keeping things running as they are: "No new commands from above? Keep up business as usual!" In other words, the pyramid matched internal stability with external stability. A match made in the Elysian Fields!

Today though, most organizations operate in environments that are anything but stable. New competitors, business models, and technologies pop up every week, with the losers in this grand competition vanishing just as quickly. And while the pyramid model can be fast and efficient when it comes to executing plans, it's painfully slow when it faces change and must adapt. This means that it's simply not suited for the hectic times companies find themselves in today.

What makes a pyramid so slow?

When something changes in an organization's environment, it's usually not the CEO who spots it first. Rather, the first people to notice are typically the ones on the ground, because they are closest to the action. These are the salespeople, customer service reps, mechanics, nurses, waiters, drivers, cashiers and so forth who form the interface between the company and its environment. These "sensors" communicate the perceived change up the chain of command, and the impulse for change must then make a slow journey up to the top of the pyramid. Only then can a decision be made, which then has to trickle back down before any actual behavioral change happens in the organization. Needless to say, this is slow going, and it's good neither for the organization nor for empowering the people working within it.

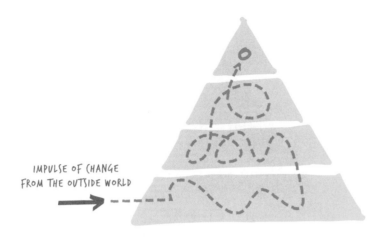

IMPULSE OF CHANGE
FROM THE OUTSIDE WORLD

Employees want responsibility

In a classical hierarchy, employees have a simple role: they execute the orders given to them by those above. They have a clearly defined zone within which they operate, and everything to the right or left of them in the pyramid is none of their concern.

In the constantly changing environment of today, organizations need well-educated employees who can detect and respond to change. In other words, they need people who are alert enough to spot opportunities and threats, and also do something about them. And to be able to abble to do this in the long run, employees must also be willing and able to continuously learn on the job and develop new skills.

But these kinds of employees know they are in demand, and they come with demands of their own. They refuse to merely obey orders at work, wanting to instead make their own decisions and wield a real influence on what the organization does. They want to be trusted with authority, offered opportunities to grow, and given the flexibility to do what they think is best.

If an organization can't give them the environment they crave, it won't be able to attract them to work there in the first place. And in today's turbulent times, lacking such employees can mean a death sentence for a company.

Maslow's Hierarchy of Needs

Employees want something bigger

Another reason why pyramids can no longer cope is that employees increasingly want their organization to have a purpose beyond trawling for profits. The way they see it, employers should pursue a cause that carries real meaning beyond making money and act in ways that are sustainable and non-harmful to the world at large in the long run. This ties in with the previous point about how pyramids will struggle to attract the talent they need if all they offer is following orders. Similarly, young, well-educated employees are increasingly unwilling to have their work contribute to the negative social and ecological impact that many large corporations have today.

This is all the more true since these employees really do have a choice: more and more entrepreneurs are taking their responsibility toward the environment and wider society seriously, which helps them attract the cream of the crop when it comes to recruiting. At the end of the day, we should all hope that this trend continues to the point where, in a few decades from now at the latest, making money is only seen as acceptable if it doesn't come at the cost of future generations.

So with these three factors in mind, the future seems rather bleak for the hierarchical tankers of old. To put it bluntly, they have to just two options: ignore the signs, stay the course, and let the band play on until the bitter end, or boldly take on the great challenge of transformation.

A s we've seen so far, the pyramid model suffers from three big limitations:

o First, it's too cumbersome to navigate today's fast-changing environment.
o Second, it fails to attract the very high-calibre employees it so direly needs, because it doesn't offer them sufficient freedom and authority.
o Third, valuable employees are also deterred because, far from providing the motivating purpose they crave, these organizations usually rather actively harm our planet and society at large.

Clearly then, we need to find new ways to collaborate—new types of organization to house our efforts toward shared goals. So what comes next?

Whereas pyramid organizations were designed to act as efficient and intricate machines for implementing orders, we now see more of a living, network-like organization emerging. These organizations are constantly changing many of their parts simultaneously, without any central authority ordering those changes. You could say that we're moving from the age of machines to the age of organisms. To clarify what exactly we mean with this, let's look at an example:

In his influential book, *Reinventing Organizations*, Frédéric Laloux describes a new type of organization which he calls *teal.* He identified this type by studying companies that were already working differently than traditional hierarchies. In such companies, he observed three defining characteristics of teal organizations:

First, *wholeness*. This means that the members of the organization can come to work as their whole selves, without needing to uphold any kind of professional facade at work. This honesty allows them to identify and form a deep bond with the organization.

A teal organization must also have an *evolutionary purpose*, meaning a clear answer to the question of why it exists. This raison d'etre must be understood, embraced and felt across the organization, and it should serve as the organization's unchanging nucleus no matter how it evolves.

Finally, teal organizations must be *self-organized*. There are no hordes of managers prodding and guiding employees in the desired direction. Instead, each team and each person must self-organize in pursuit of the organization's purpose, determining how they can best help fulfill it.

As we mentioned before, in this book we really don't care whether an organization intends to be *teal*, *agile*, self-organized, or something else. That's because these concepts and the thoughts behind them all describe different variations of the same larger groundswell toward new kinds of organization that are more organic, versatile, and human. Toward organizations that aren't designed like machines with people as cogs, but rather envisioned as living organisms that follow evolutionary principles. Toward organizations that resemble networks of self-organizing units that don't need a CEO or steering committee to make decisions for them (though CEOs and steering committees can still exist within them). Toward organizations that follow a higher purpose and change their shape continuously to best serve that purpose. Toward organizations where people can make meaningful decisions, without sticking to a twenty-page protocol, following orders from their bosses or having to resort to politics and horse-trading to get work done.

If this sounds like an inspiring vision, we're right there with you. We wholeheartedly support the idea that the organizations of the future should be purpose-driven and human-focused. But, we do want to point out one often overlooked point: at the end of the day, the goal of every transformation is for the organization to be become more *effective*, meaning to survive and thrive in its environment. What that means in terms of the organization's nature, whether friendly and warm or harsh and cold, is just a means to this end. Luckily, we live in times where effectiveness can be boosted by adopting a purpose and a human approach.

WHAT'S MISSING

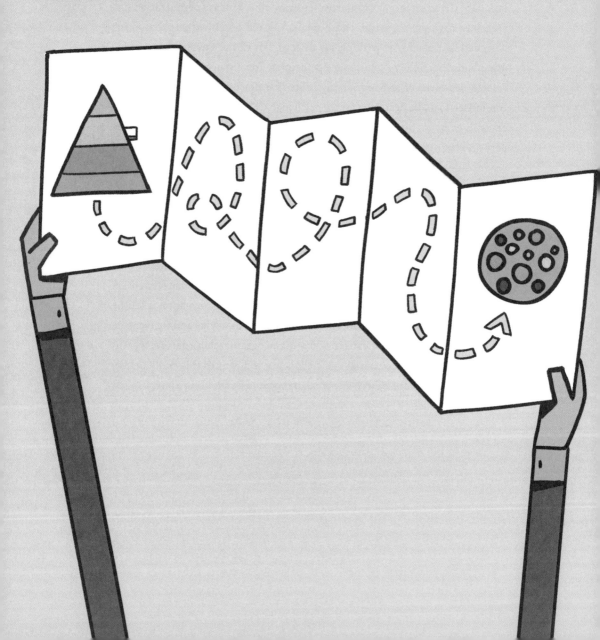

Many organizations have already seen the writing on the wall and understand that they must transform or perish. Most of them are frantically searching for the *one* right solution for what the organization of the future should look like. But this solution doesn't exist. The future of work will look different everywhere, so every organization will need its own, customized operating system to survive. So the question then becomes: how can they transform toward these new, tailor-made systems?

The answer remains elusive, especially for big, established companies that are founded on the notion that the pyramid is the only possible model. While most of them have already understood that this change is needed, they feel helpless and overwhelmed by the question of how to make it happen.

And there are no proven answers yet. This is why we created the Loop Approach: to help all kinds of organizations find their own answers.

The Loop Approach can help organizations identify practices suitable for the future of work, as well as allow them to develop their own operating systems. It provides a framework for individuals and teams to make the decisions and implement the small changes which, together, add up to a major transformation. Meanwhile, it also brings order to the tempest of "new work" tools, concept and buzzwords that are being flung around at the moment.

We unfortunately can't give you any easy answers, but we can offer a process that lets you manage a transformation that could easily turn into utter and unpredictable chaos otherwise.

What our clients often expect

In general, large organizations have one big, obvious problem when it comes to effecting substantial change: their size. If a company has tens of thousands of employees, introducing a new organizational operating system is guaranteed to be costly, high-effort, and will almost certainly lead to *a drop* in effectiveness at first.

This is why many of the big players shy away from substantial change and prefer to dabble instead by booking a few workshops, sending some employees to design thinking classes, and putting up posters with agility principles on their coffee room walls. And while all these initiatives can be helpful (except for the posters, which never work), they just won't lead to any greater transformation by themselves.

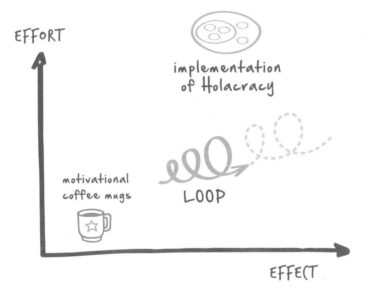

The Loop Approach is a toolkit that aims to allow organizations to transform themselves in a way that doesn't hurt their business and won't overwhelm them with a sudden, sweeping change. It provides the means to make changes and replace behaviors where updates are needed, while still retaining everything that works and should be continued.

The Loop Approach proceeds step by step, changing one behavior in one team at a time. To do so, it uses and has to use all the experience and knowledge already in the organization.

There's no one-size-fits-all solution

Whenever we begin a larger transformation project with a client, we often run into the same conflict: they expect a standard, foreseeable transformation process and a clearly-defined vision of the end result. After all, this is what they've always gotten when they've worked on transformation projects with the likes of McKinsey and BCG.

Happily, what often follows in our case is a process during which the client realizes that transformation isn't linear or predictable, so what is needed is rather a framework where it can happen in an evolutionary fashion. And while we can determine the best next step, we can't predict the best one after that. Extrapolate this over the next few years, and you might as well use a crystal ball or tarot cards to try to foresee where the organization will wind up.

Eventually, clients also tend to understand that transforming the mindset of an organization cannot be a completely *top-down* process. It can only happen in a quasi-organic way, where many short steps are taken and many small decisions made by the capable and competent people already present in the organization. In other words, the mindset is transformed through a process which already evidences the very mindset we're trying to instill.

And we too want to change our clients' mindsets, away from the the old: "This is our final destination [furious scribbling on a whiteboard], now let's figure out how to get there!" Instead, we want the expectation to be: "We don't know where exactly we'll end up, but let's just get going and learn more as we make our way"

At first glance, this might sound like we're chucking any and all clearly-defined processes and structures overboard. But in fact, we're doing the opposite: the Loop Approach is precisely a process for clearly defining how decision-making in organizations works, it just makes no predictions as to what the situation will be in a year's time. It allows for continuous small adjustments while ensuring that the right questions get asked along the way.

Based on our own experiences, this balance between standardization and flexibility is the recipe for a successful transformation.

We believe that the world sorely needs new, better organizations to be able to surmount the great challenges it faces this century. It's plain to see what harm is being inflicted on the world by pyramid organizations that exist solely to generate value for shareholders.

It's time for a change. It's time for organizations that are focused on people, not profits, and that contribute to a better future for all of us. And that's really the ultimate purpose of this book: to help bring about a better world through better organizations.

So thank you for sharing this cause with us, we're thrilled to be a part of this massive transformation with you! The world of organizations will never be the same again.

We hope that by now, the intentions behind the Loop Approach are clear to you. In the next chapter, we'll take a look at the sources underlying the Loop Approach, as well as the mindset it's built on.

It's time for a new type of organization. What you choose to call it is irrelevant.

The old *predict-and-control* paradigm is being replaced by a new *sense-and-respond* mindset.

This transformation is often painful, especially for larger, older organizations.

What is needed is a toolkit that allows them to structure the process without even pretending to offer a one-size-fits-all solution.

This toolkit should focus more on the *How*, meaning the actual transformation, rather than the *What*, meaning the organizational model it aims for.

Every organization needs to find its own operating system, and the aim of the Loop Approach is to help do exactly that.

We didn't develop the Loop Approach in a vacuum. Rather, we stood on the shoulders of giants who had already made profound contributions to the future of organizations before us, drawing on their many insights and profound thoughts.

1. From these foundations, we have distilled a certain mindset that runs through everything we do like a golden thread. It is this mindset that we wish to encourage the organizations we work with to adopt.
2. To enable you to use the Loop Approach and successfully instill that mindset, we will use this chapter to introduce our key sources, ranging from inspiring theories to concrete tools we put to use. Then, from these sources, we will deduce the main principles that we believe comprise the mindset of the organization of the future.

Over the next pages, we're going to try something pretty ambitious: briefly summarize the key concepts and schools of thought that we've built the Loop Approach upon. We acknowledge that each one is of tremendous value even by itself, and we know that we can't possibly convey them comprehensively or do them real justice with mere one-page summaries. In fact, each one would easily warrant a week of training complemented by several books, and even then you'd only be scratching the surface of their significance.

Nevertheless, for now, it's enough for you to get a brief overview of the ideas that The Loop Approach was inspired by and built upon. But if you're ambition is to become a Loop Master one day, you'll surely want to dive deeper into all or some of these concepts later on.

Why these concepts?

Of course, there are countless tools, models, frameworks, concepts, methods, and paradigms that would all be useful in the context of organizational development and transformation. And while we certainly can't claim to know all of them, we have tried and tested a fair share both ourselves and in our work with other organizations. Through a process of keeping what proved useful and discarding what didn't, we ended up with a relatively short list of tools and theories that we use in our work. Each of them has played a significant part in the development of the Loop Approach. And we're reasonably confident that the ones covered should already be enough to solve most of the organizational challenges we described in the previous part of the book.

To keep things simple, we'll answer two questions for each concept:

Why do we need this?
What are the key elements?

If you already know all these tools and theories in detail, then kudos—feel free to just skim the headlines and give yourself a pat on the back!

Holacracy

Why do we need this?

Holacracy is based on sociocracy and shares many of its key features. It is perhaps best described as software for humans, and hence for organizations too. The main idea is that authority is distributed through an organization by establishing a clear set of rules—the constitution—that everyone commits to play by.

What are the key elements?

In its constitution (which you can easily find at https://www.holacracy.org/constitution), Holacracy defines the key features of an organization. These include things like how accountabilities are packaged into roles and how decisions are made in clearly-defined meetings dictated by clearly-defined rules. So at first sight, Holacracy just seems like a set of rules. But if you look more closely, you'll find a whole new vision of what the organization of the future could look like. And while Holacracy doesn't directly answer all possible questions that an organization could run into, like how to solve conflicts or set goals, it does allow you to evolve additional processes and install them as *apps* into Holacracy itself. Brian Robertson, who originally developed Holacracy, intended it to be a complete, all-encompassing operating system that needs to be implemented fully and comprehensively to be beneficial. A bit like you can't build a ship with only some of the hull. However, we believe (and hope Brian doesn't mind us saying so) that Holacracy is also a great toolbox from which individual elements can be plucked and successfully used in other contexts, too.

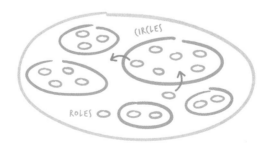

Getting Things Done

Why do we need this?

Getting Things Done, or GTD for short, was developed as a system for the self-organization of individuals. David Allen's iconic book of the same name introduces this system along with the sub-title "The Art of Stress-Free Productivity." The goal is to allow you to manage multiple projects and commitments simultaneously, while still retaining a sense of control over everything. GTD does this by helping you prioritize and align your daily tasks with your long-term goals. Its core promise is to enable individuals to navigate this complex, ever-changing world without suffering from stress and frustration.

What are the key elements?

GTD offers a complete system for reflecting on various *Horizons of Focus*. These are like different altitudes or time-frames for examining your life: What do I want to achieve in my life? What do I want to accomplish this year? Which projects will I focus on in this week? What is my next action for this project?

Happily, GTD also offers something profoundly useful in the context of working with others in teams as opposed to by oneself. That is, a shared language for work. Specifically, GTD lets us define:

○ what tasks are and how we communicate about them
○ how we define smaller and bigger projects
○ how we track commitments in a clear, unambiguous way

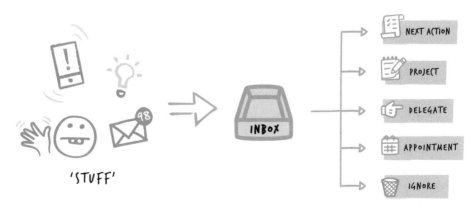

The 7 Habits of Highly Effective People

CIRCLE OF CONCERN

CIRCLE OF INFLUENCE

WHAT CAN I
CHANGE
RIGHT NOW?

proactive
Mindset

reactive
Mindset

Why do we need this?

The way we understand Stephen Covey's iconic self-help book, *The 7 Habits of Highly Effective People*, he was trying to answer the following question: What makes people effective? The book is based on the assumption that there are certain behavior patterns and belief systems that allow individuals to interact with others in more fruitful ways, enabling said individuals to have more impact on others and the world at large. One central idea is that you should focus on your *circle of influence*, aiming to be proactive and solution-oriented in things that are within your control, rather than focusing on the problems and worries that you can't do anything about.

What are the key elements?

1. **Be proactive.** Cast aside your reactive mindset and adopt one where you're the one making decisions and shaping your reality.
2. **Begin with the end in mind**. Always start with the question: "What do I want to achieve at the end of this undertaking?"
3. **Put first things first.** In any given situation, prioritize what needs to be done and start with what's most important.
4. **Think win-win.** Always look for shared successes. Covey encourages you to get out of the zero-sum mindset and rather find a way for everyone to benefit.
5. **Seek first to understand, then to be understood.** Before you jump in to share your own thoughts, ensure that you first fully understand the perspectives of others.
6. **Synergize.** Create situations where the whole is more than the sum of its parts. Ask yourself: "Where can synergies help me save time and energy?"
7. **Sharpen the saw.** Life is a marathon. To foster continuous growth and creativity, it's important to plan and actively make time for rest and relaxation.

Nonviolent communication

Why do we need this?

Nonviolent communication, or NVC for short, is a model for human-centric communication that's based on our needs. Also called the Rosenberg Model after its developer, Marshal D. Rosenberg, this framework helps you form stronger connections with others, thereby creating more robust relationships where conflicts are resolved in more constructive ways. In the context of everyday life, NVC allows you to understand your own emotions and those of others more clearly.

What are the key elements?

NVC enables people to deconstruct and resolve complex interpersonal problems. It does so by offering relatively simple tools that add a whole new layer to your communication style, making it much more effective. Among others, NVC answers the following questions:

- How can I distinguish between an observation and my own interpretation of it?
- What feelings does the behavior of someone else trigger in me? Which of my human needs are impacted in any given situation?
- How can I communicate to someone so that they fully understand and sympathize with what I say?
- How can I communicate a request so that it isn't a demand and respects the autonomy and freedom of the other person?

 INEFFECTIVE

⊘ BETTER

INTERPRETATION

'You ignore me'

OBSERVATION

'You haven't responded
to my last e-mail'

HIDDEN JUDGEMENT

'I feel disregarded'

FEELING / EMOTION

'That makes me feel
frustrated and angry'

STRATEGY

'If you don't answer,
I won't write to you
ever again.'

NEED

'I want to be respected
and make good use of
my time'

DEMAND

'I want you to
respect me more!'

REQUEST

'Would you be willing to
promise me to always
answer the same day?'

Design Thinking

Why do we need this?

Design Thinking was developed as a creative, human- and user-centric approach to complex problem solving. In its essence, it's about looking at problems with a completely open mind and deferring judgment. It offers a wide variety of methods and perspectives for examining problems, generatig ideas for solutions, testing them, and either dismissing them without judgment or pursuing them if warranted by the results.

What are the key elements?

Say the words "Design Thinking," and most people think of post-its, movable furniture, and prototypes built with Lego or sculpting clay. And indeed, all of these elements belong in a Design Thinker's toolbox, but for us, they're just means to an end. We see Design Thinking as primarily a mindset. A mindset that allows as many creative ideas as possible to emerge, helps people set their egos aside, and keeps relentless focus on these central questions:

- What problem are we trying to solve?
- How can we find useful perspectives on this problem?
- How can we test our ideas as quickly and in the most realistic context as possible?

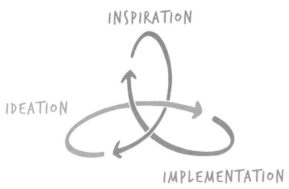

Agile methods (such as Scrum)

Why do we need this?

Originally developed for software development, Agile methods like Scrum are displacing the old waterfall planning method of: "First we do this, then that, then that…" The new style exemplifies a mindset shift away from "predict-and-control" and toward "sense-and-respond." Though implemented in teams, Scrum enables entire organizations to navigate in an ever-changing environment and deal with the complex problems that inevitably and continuously arise.

What are the key elements?

- The work happens in short, distinct sprint cycles. Each sprint ends with a "retrospective" meeting where the team reflects on and adapts the process for the next sprint.
- Teams include a role that's responsible for the product, and a scrum master role that's responsible for the sprint process used for building it.
- Teams are self-organizing and self-sufficient, meaning they don't need any outside resources to get their work done.
- Teams capture all unfinished tasks that might be tackled later in dynamic lists called backlogs.
- Plans are made in terms of distinct product features that are to be built one after another.

Even though originally intended for software development, the principles of Scrum are often used in a wide variety of other contexts, too.

Systemic Organizational Development

Why do we need this?

This practice can be seen as the antithesis of the traditional management consulting approach used by the McKinseys of the world. Systemic Organizational Development is based on the idea that consulting work should be considered akin to an intervention into a complex, living system. With this in mind, it should aim at strengthening the system by giving the right impulses for change. This is due to the assumption that complex systems can only change from within. In other words, the role of an external consultant can only ever be to help strengthen the innate problem-solving capability of the system itself.

What are the key elements?

Some of the key principles underlying Systemic Organizational Development are that you should:

- Trust the system, its ability to self-organize and find solutions to challenges, while also valuing the existing expertise.
- Be aware of interdependencies both within and between systems. Complex interactions are constantly occurring, hence no outcome can really be traced back to any single individual.
- Find the right balance between preservation and change. After all, the status quo isn't all bad. Identify the biggest pains of the organization, but at the same time value and protect what's working well already.

- Successful change means working on both the outside and inside. Organizations exist on many different levels simultaneously, and they all have to be taken into account in change efforts. The image of integral matrix above showcases these levels.

- Embrace paradoxes. Allow seeming contradictions to co-exist. For example, it's possible for an organization to be both hierarchical and agile at the same time. By embracing these paradoxes, you can gain new perspectives and find win-win solutions in almost every situation. Think "both/and" instead of "either/or."

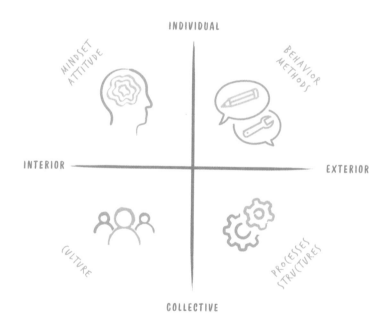

Mindfulness practices

Why do we need this?

The success of schemes like *Search Inside Yourself* clearly illustrates that mindfulness isn't just a niche hobby for people hoping to levitate anymore— it has a valuable and permanent place in the context of work, too. This new prominence is well-deserved, because the ability to view things with a certain degree of detachment helps you work more effectively both as an individual and with others. What's more, being in touch with your emotions is fast becoming recognized as one of the most essential leadership skills around. After all, you can't hope to inspire, influence, or understand others around you without understanding yourself first.

What are the key elements?

For us, mindfulness in the context of work means everything that...

- disengages our autopilot mode and breaks the stimulus-response chain-reaction that so often dominates our lives,
- grows our capacity to perceive and monitor our feelings and other mental processes,
- gives us a shared, more refined language to talk about our inner emotional lives with.

- What has got my attention?
- How am I here today?
- How do I leave?
- What do I take with me?

Positive Psychology

Why do we need this?

Whereas traditional psychology is often preoccupied with the shortcomings and pathologies of the human mind, positive psychology focuses rather on its strengths and potential. The underlying assumption of positive psychology is that people can feel intrinsically motivated to work toward a goal, and they can be inspired to feel that way. All that is needed is to nudge them a little to help them discover and make use of their full potential.

This way of thinking is well-suited to a world where employees need to make decisions under conditions of uncertainty, where roles evolve and are dynamically distributed based on who can best fulfill them, and where teams self-organize without managers who do all the hard thinking for them.

What are the key elements?

When it comes to positive psychology in the context of work, we've found the following questions the most important, which is why we regularly ask them:

- In our team, what strengths and potential does each individual bring to the table?
- How can we communicate these transparently, so that everyone is aware of each other's profiles?
- How can the potential of each person be best put to use and developed?

In general, positive psychology encourages us to look for the good in people, focusing on potential and opportunities, not shortcomings and risks.

Spiral Dynamics and Integral Theory

Why do we need this?

Frederic Laloux's landmark book *Reinventing Organizations* builds upon the key thoughts from both spiral dynamics and integral theory. These theories posit that like life on earth, our "collective" human consciousness naturally evolves towards increasingly complex states, from ruthless, short-sighted selfishness to more enlightened, "civilized" discourse. Laloux applies this same reasoning to the world of organizations: when an organization attempts to transform, it is really trying to evolve to be better-adapted to surviving in the world. A noteworthy addition is that according to Laloux, each evolutionary stage of organizations, even the more primitive ones, have their strengths and can be well-suited for specific contexts, so more evolved does not always mean better.

What are the key elements?

In *Reinventing Organizations,* Laloux describes five distinct stages of organizational development, represented by colors:

- Impulsive Red
- Conformist Amber
- Achievement Orange
- Pluralistic Green
- Evolutionary Teal

For more on these, please see the image below.

Of course, real-world organizations are so complex that they never neatly fall under any single category. So when Laloux says that an organization is orange, what he really means is that the majority of its structures, practices, and processes are in line with the orange mindset. As we've mentioned previously, Laloux calls the current, "highest" stage of organizational development *teal.* This term denotes organizations that don't resemble machines (a trait of orange organizations), but are closer to living organisms, continuously evolving and adapting.

Evolution of Organizations

ACC. TO FRÉDÉRIC LALOUX: REINVENTING ORGANIZATIONS

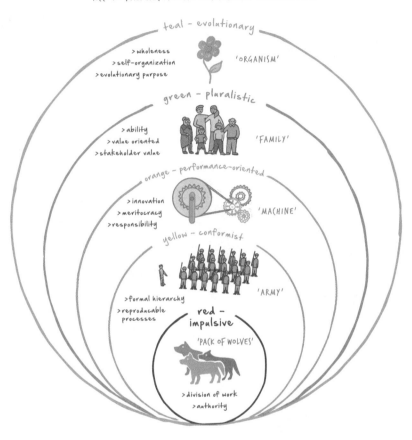

teal – evolutionary
> wholeness
> self-organization
> evolutionary purpose
'ORGANISM'

green – pluralistic
> ability
> value oriented
> stakeholder value
'FAMILY'

orange – performance-oriented
> innovation
> meritocracy
> responsibility
'MACHINE'

yellow – conformist
> formal hierarchy
> reproducable processes
'ARMY'

red – impulsive
'PACK OF WOLVES'
> division of work
> authority

→ ORGANIZATIONS ARE COLORFUL, BUT ONE COLOR IS ALWAYS PREVALENT

→ EACH STEP OF EVOLUTION MIRRORS ITS SOCIAL DEVELOPMENT

*B*y laying out all these great sources next to each other, we see some patterns of principles emerge. As different as the various tools and theories described above may seem at first glance, we've noticed in our own work with them that they do in fact share an underlying mindset. For us, this mindset is the fundamental characteristic of the organization of the future, and attaining it requires introducing certain principles into an organization that change the way people think and behave. We call this the Loop Mindset, and we'll present its constituent parts below.

Autonomy and Self-organization

While we don't know exactly what the organization of the future will look like, we are sure that autonomy and self-organization will be hard-coded into it. Each team and each role within it will be empowered to make decisions and take action quickly and autonomously. This will enable the organization to be *agile*, acting quickly and adapting whenever necessary.

Autonomy and self-organization are prerequisites for a functional sense and respond mindset to emerge. That's because an organization can only respond rapidly to changes on all fronts if the teams and people there are free to self-organize and act independently without having to wait for decisions to trickle down. Of course, the result of all this autonomy could easily be chaos and anarchy, which is why alignment becomes crucial. This brings us to our next point.

Purpose-orientation

Purpose-orientation means that, beyond goals, strategies and visions, the organization has also defined and communicated a greater purpose that it pursues. This purpose forms a strong foundation for the organization, because all members connect with it on an emotional level. The purpose not only allows people to identify with the organization, it also provides a guiding beacon that helps individuals and teams to navigate even under great uncertainty. In turbulent times, a purpose grants a measure of basic stability beyond what mere goals and strategies can provide. Of course, that's not to say that goals and strategies aren't still necessary—they are. A purpose is meant to complement, not replace, these concrete, more short-term planning tools.

Self-responsibility

We believe that every human being has the potential to own their work, make decisions, and act independently. What often holds them back is that most traditional workplaces don't trust them to be self-responsible, but rather have the higher-ups in the hierarchy take responsibility for them. This is fast becoming problematic, and we believe that full self-responsibility will be an absolute necessity in the organization of the future.

But what does "self-responsibility" mean, exactly? It's when people are able to take full responsibility for their own thoughts, feelings and actions. This attitude is exemplified by statements like "I see a tension, namely that..." or "What I need from you is ..." Unfortunately, in most organizations, such direct and constructive verbalizations are still rare.

Perhaps the most important message we want to impart with this book is that *you* are the transformation. To transform your organization, you first have to overcome certain harmful thinking patterns of your own, such as expecting your boss to change things for you. Start in your own circle of influence and make small incremental changes that gradually add up. By becoming self-responsible, you can be a role model for others, multiplying the effect. All you can do is change yourself. But luckily, that's all it takes.

Solution-orientation

In many traditional organizations, thinking tends to revolve around problems. That's because finding new solutions typically isn't rewarded, and it's not really part of most people's job descriptions. That's what the bosses are there for, and dreaming up a solution that they didn't think of is just likely to make them look bad! This is also why problem orientation is the lifeblood of politics and power games: if I can find the problem in your thinking, this will make me seem smarter by comparison, giving me an edge when the next promotion comes up.

Of course, the organization of the future lives by a completely different mindset. Sure, identifying problems and shortcomings is still important, but it's not enough by itself to warrant any kudos. Rather, this is just the starting point for the truly important work: proposing ideas for solutions. In other words, spotting the iceberg isn't enough—someone actually needs to take action to avoid it. This solution-orientation is ingrained in all the tools and theories we base the Loop Approach on, and it manifests itself in language like: "I observe the following problem ... and I propose to fix it like so ..." The good news is that rather than a complete revolution, thinking in terms of solutions can be easily added to an existing problem-oriented mindset, like an upgrade. In the course of this book, we'll give you the tools for doing so.

Thinking win-win

In traditional organizations, the standard type of thinking is "either/or," whereas what is needed today is more of a "both … and" mindset. Succeeding in complex environments requires cooperation, and this only happens when the solutions sought are seen as a win-win, satisfying all stakeholders. Instead of a solution where either you or I win, we should find one where *both* you *and* I win. That's because succeeding in complex environments requires cooperation, and this only happens when the solutions sought are seen as a win-win, satisfying all stakeholders.

While the silos in old organizations encouraged people to focus on their own team's gains, in network-like ones, everyone must seek shared successes, including with external partners. The shared purpose ought to drive everyone's work, encouraging cooperation to that end instead of flying elbows and bloody noses in a mad scramble for the biggest slice of the pie.

Transparency and open communication

In traditional organizations, information is power, which is why it's often purposely hidden: "You want to know something? I know where you can find it, but first you have to do something for me." But now, we see this mindset being replaced by one of *radical transparency*, where everything and anything going on in the organization is freely and openly shared. This shift is necessary because in complex systems, it's hard to predict what information will be needed where, when, and by whom. Thus, the only effective solution is to make all information freely accessible at anytime. Hand-in-hand with this goes the cultural shift away from "we talk *about* each other" to "we talk *with* each other." In a network where everyone is connected to everyone, open and honest feedback becomes increasingly important both for the effectiveness of those innumerable one-on-one relationships, but also to help maintain a warm, pleasant working environment.

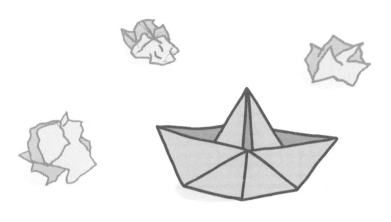

Thinking in continuous iterations

The mantra that captures the essence of this principle is "Shipped is better than perfect." That's because, in a complex world, constant experiments and relentless incremental progress win the day. When the environment keeps changing, no solution can be perfect in the long run, meaning it's best to strive for incremental improvements that work here and now. Rather than asking if something is the perfect solution, the right attitude is "Is this going to cause any permanent harm? No? Then, please hold my pre-meeting Moscow Mule, and let's try it!"

This principle is especially prominent in Design Thinking, but in fact, it's present in all the tools and theories relevant to organization and collaboration. Just consider Holacracy with its continuous governance process and the idea to constantly ask of new initiatives: "Is it safe enough to give it a try?"

Role vs. soul

Whereas in the past, a person and the job they performed were broadly considered inseparable, we now see organizations embrace a different kind of thinking, where people are seen as separate entities from the roles they fulfill. Though this distinction may seem like a technicality, it actually provides a host of benefits. Perhaps the most important advantage is that authority can be distributed much more flexibly in the organization. For instance, one person can fulfill different roles in different meetings, as well as pick up new roles as they appear or drop old ones when they're no longer relevant. Whereas previously the boss was the boss, no matter what the meeting, they can now, in theory, take both a lead role and a supporting role, depending on the context. The person leading the marketing team could simultaneously hold the role responsible for watering plants around the office under the lead of the office manager role.

Ego to Self

This is another principle that we see in many of the tools and theories underlying the Loop Approach. Whereas in the world of pyramids, people's egos constantly clash in the fight to rise up in the ranks, we now see organizations value a transition from "Ego to Self." This means that people leave their egos behind to serve the organization's higher purpose. This is not only more effective in the big picture, it also fosters the humility people need to take on the challenge of understanding themselves as human beings. This is important in a complex system where these intelligent sensors must constantly interact, and therefore need a deep understanding of how they work and tick. They must come to accept themselves so that they can truly focus on harnessing and developing their strengths for the greater good, rather than trying to manage impressions and maneuver themselves into pole position for the next promotion.

Tension-based work

For us, this is perhaps one of the most central tenets of new organizations. When everyone in the organization takes responsibility for sensing information, they will also spot tensions, meaning areas where something in the organization could be done differently than it currently is. These tensions can then be translated into real problems to solve and questions to ask, and eventually into new ideas and proposals which will drive all kinds of meaningful change in the organization. Just like physical tensions in your muscles, tensions start out as simple feelings that people have. But they can lead to real changes, and in fact, they will become the engine for driving the continuous improvement process that is needed today. That's why an effective organization needs good tools to make tensions explicit and visible, as well as to then resolve them by turning them into meaningful change. The old system of grumbling under one's breath, snapping pencils in half, and occasionally letting someone know what you really think of them at an office party just won't cut it anymore.

Distributed leadership

In the past, the distinction between leaders and employees was crystal clear, and even reinforced through things like parking spaces, big desks, and other perks. But today, these lines are fast becoming blurred, and in the organization of the future, anyone can lead—both themselves and others. This new kind of leadership arises thanks to roles: when someone has a role and the authority and expertise that go with it, that person can lead others simply by taking responsibility and making decisions. Of course, this distribution increases complexity, because who the leader is will depend on the situation and topic at hand. But it also makes an organization much more effective, because experts who have the relevant knowledge are embedded everywhere, capable of making quick decisions within their own areas of responsibility. As the environment is constantly churning, not even the most all-knowing, God-like manager could hope to keep making the right decisions in the right places at the right times all alone.

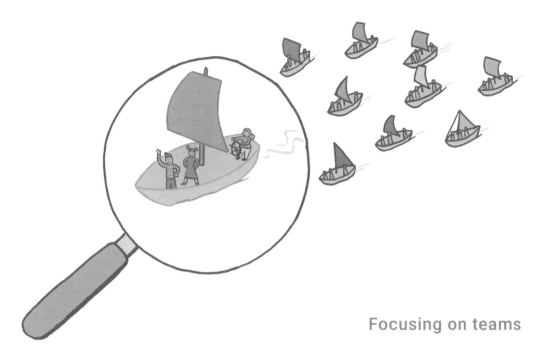

Focusing on teams

The way we see it, effective organizations are mostly just a sum of the teams within them. That's why, if you want to change an organization, you need to change the teams that it is comprised of. In other words, you have to change the way people interact in those teams, meaning the way they work together. This is accomplished by introducing new tools and practices that encourage collaboration and strengthen relationships. And when you have strong teams, a strong organization is not far behind. This is why strengthening and evolving teams is one of the main points in the Loop Approach.

THE KEY TAKEAWAYS FROM THIS CHAPTER:

There are many tools and theories that
we've drawn on to create the Loop Approach

Many of them share a certain
mindset.

This mindset is the core characteristic of the
organization of the future, which is why we aim
to instill it in the organizations we work with.

PART 2

THE LOOP APPROACH

Welcome to the main part of the book. Now it's time to get our hands dirty and learn how to transform an organization using the Loop Approach. The three chapters that follow will each convey a necessary building block for doing so:

1   Chapter one introduces our framework for organizational effectiveness: *The 7 Habits of Highly Effective Organizations*. This framework allows us to measure where an organization is right now in terms of effectiveness and then decide which direction it should evolve in.

2   Chapter two delves into the heart of the Loop Approach: *the Loop*, a team-based change curriculum. The Loop is how we change the behavior inside an organization, team-by-team.

3   Chapter three zooms out to the bigger picture by providing a broader *transformation architecture*. Here you'll learn which work streams are needed in addition to the Loops to extend the transformation beyond

THE 7 HABITS

W e've covered where the Loop Approach comes from, but now it's time to dive into the approach itself and introduce its first element: The 7 Habits of Highly Effective Organizations.

We've repeatedly seen the need for this tool in our work with clients, because we've found that we can't even begin to talk about any kind of transformation unless we have...

- a shared view on where the organization is right now,
- a shared understanding of the biggest current pain points,
- a shared vision of the desired direction for the transformation and what success would look like.

These criteria can only be fulfilled if you have some framework for describing effective organizations, meaning a shared yardstick that measures where an organization is right now and allows you to define the direction it should move in. Since the goal of every transformation is to become more effective, this framework needs to break down the key components of effectiveness into usable dimensions. We call these components "habits," since each one describes a broad cluster of behaviors that contribute to an organization's effectiveness.

The 7 Habits framework allows us to:

- Define precisely what effectiveness means in a given organization, along seven distinct dimensions of effectiveness.
- Measure the status quo, meaning where an organization is along each of those seven dimensions.
- Define an ideal target state or "habit" toward which a transformation should proceed, thereby making it possible to identify the next evolutionary step for each dimension.

The above three steps result in a strong foundation for transformation.

Clear alignment

The first habit of effective organizations is clear alignment. An organization can only be effective if everybody knows exactly which way it's going so that they can help. Alignment requires clearly defining and communicating purpose, strategies, and goals through-out the organization.

Fully-used potential

The second habit means that the full scope of potential inside a team and the organization in general is made visible and put to good use. This primarily has to do with the potential of each person inside the team, with the goal having an understanding of who brings what skills and strengths to the table, and how they can best be put to use.

Distributed authority

The third habit builds on the second: if the skills and full potential of each team member are known, they should be matched with the right roles and accountabilities inside the organization. And, of course, for these roles to be successful, they also need to have the authority to make decisions.

Individual effectiveness

The fourth habit is to strive for individual effectiveness. For a team or organization to be able to self-organize its work, each individual within it must be able to do the same. This habit means asking questions like: Are the people in an organization truly filling their roles effectively? Are they, as individuals, capable of translating their accountabilities into results? Do they have the right tools and use the right practices to do so?

Team effectiveness

The fifth habit builds on the fourth: even if individuals are able to self-organize, the same must be true of the team they find themselves in. To see if this is the case, the following questions are helpful: Are teams able to coordinate and communicate effectively? Do they have good meeting routines, so that people draw energy and insights from them, rather than being drained by them? Do teams find ways to self-organize around their shared goals and purpose? Do they possess the right tools and practices to do so?

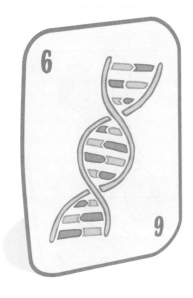

High adaptability

The sixth habit has to do with the perpetual development of an organization. In turbulent environments, an effective organization must constantly shapeshift, like an octopus squeezing its way through a drainpipe. This requires championing a mindset of neverending change and improvement. The habit can best be analyzed through questions like: Are teams and the organization as a whole able to continuously evolve, changing their structure and rules to adapt to changing circumstances? Do they learn and change along the way?

Conflict & feedback competence

The seventh and final habit is closely connected to the sixth: just as the organization must continue to evolve, so too must the people within it. In fact, an organization can only be effective if, first, people are hungry to learn from their experiences as well as the constant feedback that they should be receiving. And second, if people can resolve their conflicts in ways that strengthens the parties involved and the team as a whole.

Clarity, Results, Evolution

Congratulations, you've already learned about one key element of the Loop Approach: The 7 Habits of Effective Organizations. But to actually make those habits a reality, we need the Loop, which forms the backbone of the Loop Approach.

First, let's group those seven habits into three broader themes: Clarity, Results, and Evolution. These themes form a loop, which an effective organization, as well as every team within it, cycles through continuously.

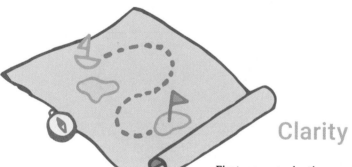

Clarity

First, an organization needs to create clarity by thinking about questions like: Who are we and what are we trying to accomplish? How will we navigate so that we get there? What is the potential of the team and everyone in it? How can we best use everyone's potential, matching with it with the right roles and accountabilities?

Results

Once an organization has clarity, this clarity needs to be translated into the desired results. This usually comes from answering the following questions: How can we ensure that each of us is self-organized in an effective way? How can we as a team take the clarity we've attained and then work together effectively toward our shared goal, producing meaningful results in the process?

Evolution

Working on the results invariably creates tensions and conflict. But this isn't a bad thing: resolving them drives continuous improvement and evolution. This in turn necessitates a new phase of seeking clarity, thereby starting a fresh loop.

In the next part of this book, we'll show you how to use the Loop Approach as a base from which to launch a transformation. It's fundamentally a team-based approach, where each team goes through the three modules of Clarity, Results, and Evolution in endless iterations, becoming more effective each time. This means that a successful transformation cant't be defined as getting from A to B, because the process never really ends.

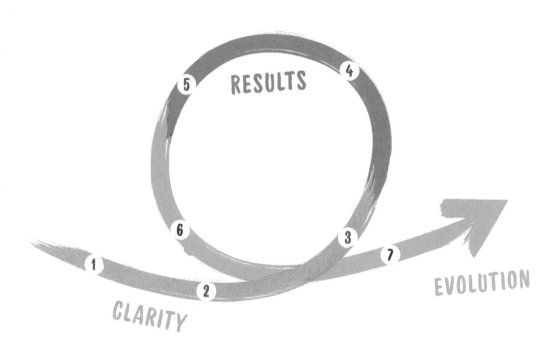

1 CLEAR ALIGNMENT

2 FULLY USED POTENTIAL

3 DISTRIBUTED AUTHORITY

4 INDIVIDUAL EFFECTIVENESS

5 TEAM EFFECTIVENESS

6 HIGH ADAPTABILITY

7 CONFLICT & FEEDBACK
  COMPETENCE

The 7 Habits of Highly Effective Organization form the first element of the Loop Approach. They are:

1. **Clear alignment**
2. **Fully used potential**
3. **Distributed authority**
4. **Individual effectiveness**
5. **Team effectiveness**
6. **High adaptability**
7. **Conflict & feedback competence**

The seven habits can be grouped into the three broader themes that comprise the Loop: *Clarity, Results, and Evolution*

This Loop is the base for our team-based curriculum for organizational transformation. You'll learn all about this in the next part of the book

LOOP

A

MODULE 2

START

D

C

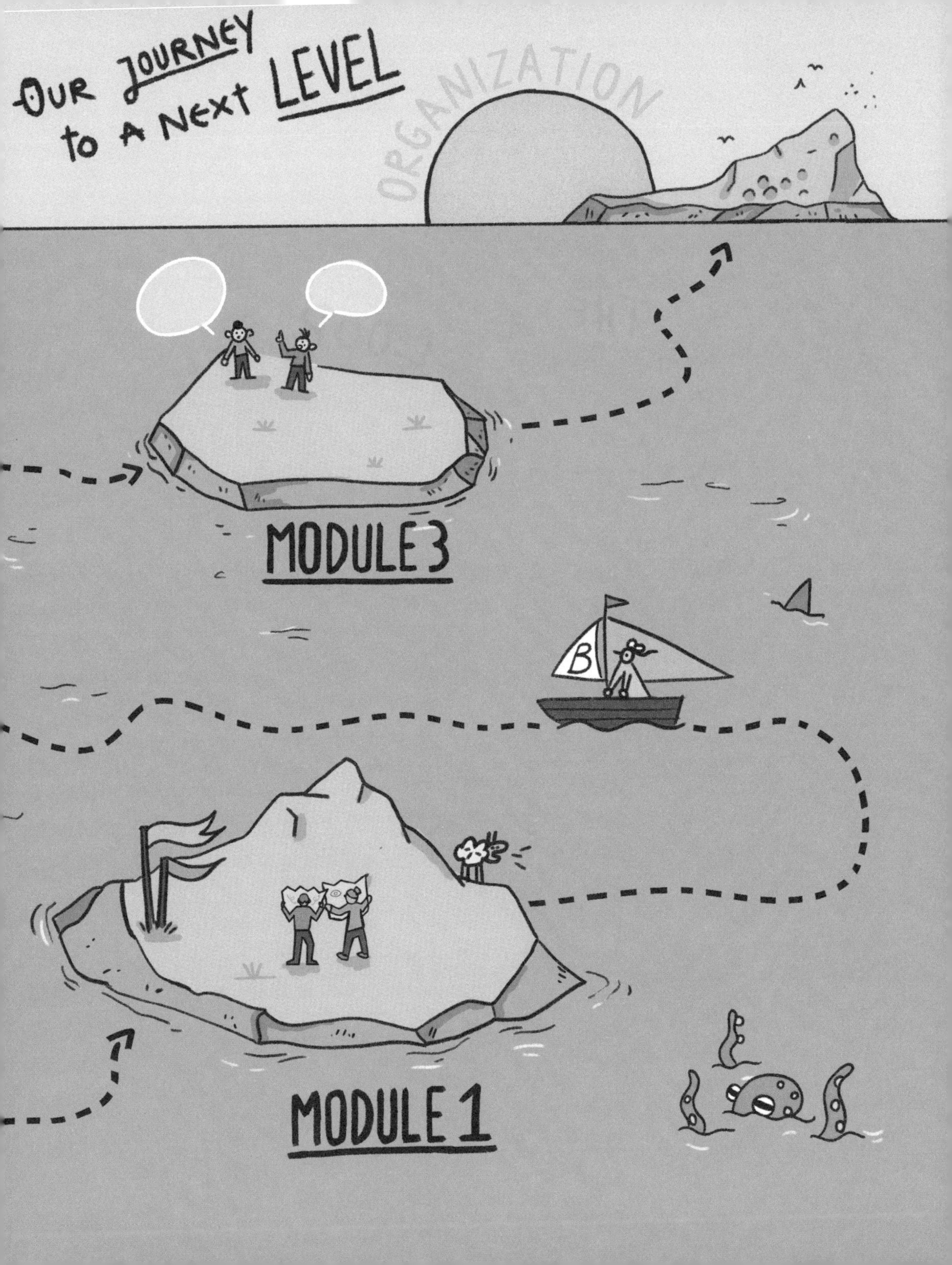

Our JOURNEY to a Next LEVEL
ORGANIZATION
MODULE 3
B
MODULE 1

THE LOOP

We've finally arrived at the eponymous Loop of the Loop Approach, our team-based transformation program. Its goal is to fundamentally transform the work of a single team, modifying all aspects of how team members think and talk about work. We'll use the 7 Habits of Highly Effective Organizations to examine every aspect of a team's work and ask: "Where will our future organization be different? Where should we make changes today?"

But why did we choose to put all this emphasis on teams? Quite simply, because this is where the real work happens. At their core, effective organizations are just a collection of effective teams that are aligned well.

Another key aspect of our transformation program is that it focuses on changing behavior. An organization is the behavior it exhibits, and its culture is the principles that manifest in its collective behavior. We can talk about culture and mindset all we want, but what we really want to see in the end is concrete behavioral change.

One last point: when we talk about behavior, we tend to focus specifically on the language used in a team. That's because almost everything that happens in an organization today is really, at its base, communication: conveying information from one person to another.

In the Loop program, you'll find three modules: Clarity, Results, and Evolution. Every team that embarks on the program will start a transformation journey toward the next level of work, and this journey has been perhaps best visualized by one on our clients in the image below:

The modules build on one another, and typically they each take the form of a two-day workshop. In this part of the book, you'll learn what a journey through all three modules would typically look like.

CLARITY

Clarity is the prerequisite and foundation for good work. That's why we dedicate the first module of every transformation to the topic, so that the team can create a shared base for self-organizing their work later on. They do this by defining goals and a purpose for themselves, examining what exactly everyone does at work every day as well as understanding the competencies and skills that each team member brings to the table.

Module 1 comprises the following three components, each aiming to answer a broad question:

1 **Alignment:** Why does this team exist, and what is its higher purpose?
2 **People's Potential:** What skills and capabilities are available in the team?
3 **Accountability:** How is responsibility broken down into roles within the team?

We usually consider the Module 1 workshop to have been a success if by the end of it…

- ☐ the team has understood what the Loop Approach is and what its building blocks are,
- ☐ the team has defined and documented its purpose, as well as goals for the near and mid-term future,
- ☐ the strengths and potential of each team member have been identified and made transparent throughout the team. And in the process, the team members have gotten to know each other a little better and formed stronger connections.
- ☐ each team-member knows their areas of responsibility in the team and has packaged them into roles. Those roles have been made transparent and are clearly distinct from one another,
- ☐ the team has understood the concept of tensions and started applying it to their daily work.

Clear alignment: Why does this team exist, what is it needed for?

The first building block of clarity is alignment around a shared Why. In this first part of the module, the team will learn how to work with tensions and find and verbalize a shared purpose.

WORKING WITH TENSIONS

Though the Loop Approach is modular and fairly flexible, one absolutely none-negotiable requirement is that the team develop a competency for working with tensions. Each individual must be able to consistently identify and raise tensions, as well as solve them alone or with others. This skill is crucial for the team's journey through the three modules. Our approach is to provide a basic structure, which the team must be able to then adapt and complement. But to do so, they need to raise tensions in the form of questions and suggestions. Based on these, we revise the agenda of the workshop to help the team make the most of it.

For us, a tension is defined as the gap between what is and what could be. It doesn't have a negative connotation, but rather serves as a positive impulse for change, a signal of unused potential that can be harnessed. But we can only put that potential to use if someone raises the tension. And this is actually an important part of the concept of tensions: they are always things that are present in and felt by *a person*. A team or organization can't feel tensions. That's why individuals carry the responsibility of sensing and raising them, which is also why, when capturing tensions, we make note of *whose* tensions they are.

To ensure that all tensions are captured, early in the workshop, we introduce an open agenda, a "tension stash". Everyone can use the agenda during the workshop by writing down tensions on post-its, jotting down just a word or two along with their name. Then, the stash is periodically emptied in slots reserved expressly for dealing with tensions. This way, participants don't need to keep them in mind, and the flow of the workshop won't be derailed by dozens of spontaneous discussions.

TENSIONS

THE FUEL OF THE ORGANIZATION

TENSIONS ARE: IDEAS   WISHES   NEEDS

    POTENTIALS FOR IMPROVEMENT   STROKES OF GENIUS

   INSPIRATIONS   PROBLEMS   CONFLICTS ...

 Every impulse for change

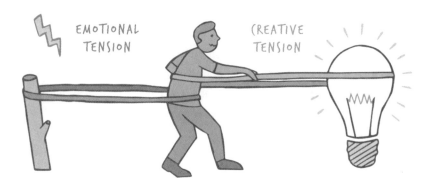

EMOTIONAL TENSION   CREATIVE TENSION

ALWAYS START WITH WHY

At this early stage in the workshop, we tend to assume that some or even most of the participants don't really fully understand why they're in the room. Hence, at this point, we take some time to explain the Why for them on multiple levels so that everyone has a clear reason for being there. To do so, we go through the same questions we covered in the first part of this book:

- What problems does the old organizational model—the pyramid—cause?
- Why is an update needed?
- What would an organization look like where each individual could harness their various strengths and full potential?
- Would employees in such an organization be creative, responsible, capable of thinking critically and connecting with others around them?
- Why are the days of the pyramid model numbeterd?
- What factors render it unable to adapt and compete with more network-like organizations?
- Why are companies modelled after pyramids losing their best talent?

You've already read a whole chapter on the answers to these questions, so we won't dive deeper into them here. But in the workshop, this part is meant to ensure that the whole team understands why change is needed, while also giving them a passing glimpse into what a new and improved organization might look like.

Once this fundamental *Why* has been answered, we switch to another Why: the purpose. By this, we mean both the purpose of the organization— why the world needs it—as well as the purpose of the team—why it is exists and why the organization needs it. Someone working in a team that's embedded in an organization needs the answers to both those *Whys* to get them out of bed every morning. In other words, they also need some awareness—however vague—of why the organization is needed and what positive impact it has on the world. Of course, in our workshops, neither we nor the team can typically do much to change the purpose of the organization, so the idea is rather to create a shared understanding of what's already there.

What we then truly focus on is the purpose of the team itself, which plays many important roles: It acts like glue, keeping the team together in a turbulent sea of external change. It's a motivating magnet that yanks people out of bed and into the office each morning. It's a compass that the team uses to navigate, especially under the thick fogs of uncertainty. When we show up at a company, this purpose often hasn't yet been made explicit. That's why, right after a quick detour in the following section, we'll explain how a team can uncover its purpose.

PURPOSE

REASON TO BE

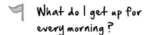 Why does the world need us?

What drives me?

What do I get up for
every morning?

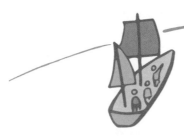

From Why To How To What

In his book *Start with Why*, Simon Sinek introduced the concept of the Golden Circle. The Golden Circle is made up of nested circles: the Why-circle at the center, the How-circle surrounding it and the What-circle encompassing both of the previous ones. To understand how this tool works in practice, let's look at the automotive company Tesla as an example.

Tesla's purpose, it's Why-circle at the heart of things, might be something like "To accelerate the advent of sustainable transport." This is the raison d'etre the company gives itself. It's their long-term, ideal goal, and it's one that might never be able to fully achieved. Once this Why is clear, the How-circle comes next: What is Tesla's strategy? What unique idea will help them move toward their purpose? In Tesla's case, their How is probably changing the common perception that electric cars are slow, hideous and impractical due to poor battery-life. Of course, there are countless ways in which this How could be attained. So what lies in Tesla's What-circle? According to the company's website, its What is to "bring [...] compelling mass market electric cars to market as soon as possible"

Why did we walk you through this example? First, to demonstrate how motivating a compelling purpose can be. Second, to show how the *Why* can and should be connected to the *How* and *What* of a company. Stacking them in this way means that the purpose can serve as a guiding beacon for employees to make coherent, meaningful decisions in everyday work. The purpose of an organization isn't just something the brand department came up with at their offsite in the Azores. If done right, the purpose really can make a difference in the organization every single day. Third, we introduced the Golden Circle as a tool here because it will prove useful in the next exercise, where we distinguish between the purpose and other useful tools for creating organizational alignment.

The Golden Circle

BY SIMON SINEK

THE PURPOSE PLAYOFFS

Let's get our hands dirty with a fun and impactful exercise! (Don't worry, this really can be fun, not like when some sadist starts a presentation with "Alright everyone, please stand up for a fun little warm-up exercise")

The idea here is to allow a team to define its purpose explicitly. By now, the team should understand what a purpose is and why it's needed. What's more, they should have at least a general idea of the organization's purpose, or if they don't, they should have added it as a tension to be resolved. In other words, they should have a strong basis to uncover the purpose of their team in the workshop.

In order to define this purpose, they ask themselves two guiding questions:

- ☐ *What are we needed for (in our organization and beyond)?*
- ☐ *What gets me out of bed every morning to to go to work?*

Since these questions could easily spark days or even weeks of soul-searching and discussion, we've created a playful and pragmatic method for verbalizing some first answers to them: The Purpose Playoffs. It consists of five steps:

❘ The Stakeholder Map

As a first step, the group creates a large mindmap illustrating all the stakeholders the team believes it creates value for. This includes individuals who interact with the team, other teams, external stakeholders like society at large or the environment, as well as the team members themselves.

To do this, participants write down on post-it notes any and all stakeholders that they create value for. In classic brainstorming style, there are no right or wrong answers, and volume is the only consideration: mass trumps class. It's even OK if some stakeholders overlap or are mentioned multiple times. The only rules are that:

- [ ] Each post-it can only denote one stakeholder or group of stakeholders. This makes it easier to rearrange them later, for example by sorting them into clusters or leaving them as a long laundry list.
- [ ] All post-its should be stuck on the wall right away, so that others can see them and be inspired by them to write more ideas.
- [ ] Discussions are forbidden at this stage and only clarifying questions (like "I can't read your handwriting") are allowed.

2 Value Clusters

As a result of the previous step, we should now have identified a large number of stakeholders, Next, we take a good hard look at them and start jotting down answers to the question "What kind of value do we create for those stakeholders?" Again, each idea is written on a post-it, which is then stuck to the wall for all to see. The list of stakeholders is only there to help spark thoughts about what kind of value is created, so it's not necessary to think of something for every stakeholder or even to spell out what value is delivered to whom. There's no discussion at this stage either, and the brainstorming continues as long as people keep finding new types of value that the team creates.

Next, the facilitator, meaning one of us trainers, starts clustering the value post-its with the help of the group. This means grouping similar aspects of value together and assigning a descriptive label to each cluster. Typically, these labels will turn out fairly abstract, because they need to capture all aspects of the post-its in the cluster. So we might wind up with labels like: "Reliability," "Empowerment," "Speed," "Warmth," and so forth.

Ideally, by the end of this step, we'll have around 5—7 labeled clusters that provide a high-level view of the different kinds of value that team creates. But we can't just tack them together and call that a purpose. We need a formulation that's motivating and meaningful.

EXERCISE: PURPOSE PLAYOFFS

GOAL:
The group finds and
verbalizes a first version
of their purpose

4 – 40
PEOPLE

2 – 5
HOURS

Post-its,
pens and
a whiteboard
or flipchart

3 Integration Playoffs

In this step, each participant writes down their definition of the team's purpose, but doesn't share it yet. Probably, the resulting sentences will be long
and convoluted, but this doesn't matter, because they'll all be discarded and
replaced with better ones by the time the day is done anyway. The goal here is
just to build the first, imperfect purpose prototypes that capture all that we've
learned in the previous steps. To gauge whether this is what's happening, it's
usually enough to check if all the value clusters from the last step are covered
by each prototype. A useful way to get people thinking in the right direction is
to have them ask themselves: "What are we needed for" and then answer with
"We…" Once someone has found a verbalisation, they can also use the Golden
Circle to try to gauge which aspects of it constitute the *Why, How* and *What*.

Then, the playoffs begin. Participants form pairs,
and everyone takes 15 minutes to explain to their partners the prototype they came up with, and vice versa.
Then both prototypes are unceremoniously discarded,
and the pair comes up with something new that still
covers all the important aspects of the team's purpose.
Importantly, both partners must agree to the new prototype. Again, they can use the Golden Circle to distinguish exactly what the actual *Why* in the statement is,
though they still keep the whole statement.

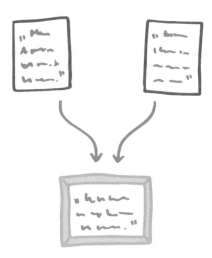

Once each pair has agreed on an updated version
of the purpose, they decide which one of them will
represent the pair in the next round. Meanwhile, the
other person will act as a spectator. They can cheer
the other person on and contribute ideas from the sidelines, but they won't
be making any actual decisions anymore. In the next round of the playoffs,
two representatives again square off, explaining their prototypes, discarding
them and creating something new. Once they've agreed on the next iteration,
they decide who will "play for the team" in the next round.

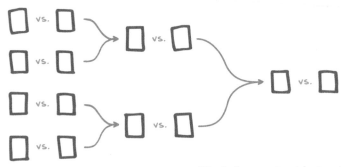

At some point, only two representatives will be left, meaning it's time for the grand finale. They present their prototypes and then try to integrate them into one last version. Once they agree, they present the resulting prototype to the group. When doing so, they should use the Golden Circle to indicate what the *Why* is, using the *How* and *What* to give it more context. Then, the group should discuss the result, integrating any tensions into the purpose.

Of course, this relatively brief exercise rarely results in an eternal, immutable purpose. But that's not the goal either. Instead, the aim is to define a prototype that everyone can live with. One that's "safe enough to try."

Purpose, Vision Strategy and Goals

- In our work, we often get asked about the difference between purpose, strategy and goals. To help explain it, we usually use the image below.
- Strategy and goals are important, and if these aspects are ailing in a team or organization, someone probably feels a major tension about it.
- The Loop Approach offers many methods for solving such a tension: A role can be established to take responsibility for strategy and goals (see Module 1) or a standard meeting can be created (see Module 3). It can also be tackled in an additional module of the Loop Approach, or as part of the leadership work-stream (see part 3 of the book).
- So even though you won't find a set of tools for goal setting and strategy crafting in this part of the book, we fully appreciate the relevance of these aspects.

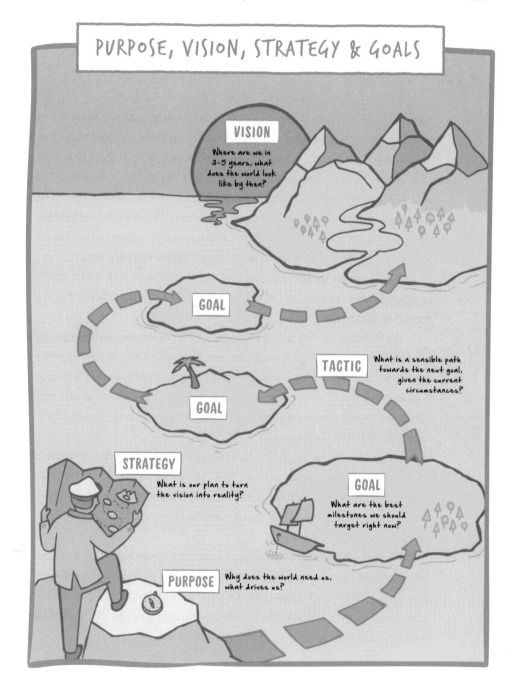

Fully-used potential: Which skills and strengths do team members bring to the table?

The first kind of clarity we seek in the Clarity module is clarity around purpose. By now, this should have been attained, as the team will have identified, verbalized and aligned on its purpose. This, in our view, is already worthy of applause. Purpose definition could easily take days of dry, exhausting and all too often fruitless discussions, but we landed on a purpose in just a few hours and might have even found ourselves having a bit of fun in the process. Even better, everyone in the room got to participate and hence feels heard. Wouldn't it be great if all work could be this enjoyable and pragmatic?

Our goal for the second building block of this module is to create transparency around the members of the team, putting a spotlight on their skills, strengths and competencies.

In the first step, we ask each team member to send a message to five people who know them particularly well. The message reads: *Can you please do me a huge favour and tell me what my three biggest strengths are? What am I particularly good at? What positive attributes do you associate with me? (Please don't ask why, I'll tell you someday, but right now I'm in the middle of a workshop called the Twist or something.)*

But why do we focus on strengths here, instead of areas to improve? Well, as economist Peter Drucker stated: "The task of leadership is to create an alignment of strengths... making a system's weaknesses irrelevant". What's more, focusing on strengths is much more motivating than zooming in on every chink in the armor.

This approach is also in line with the mindset of the organization of the future, where there are no fixed jobs, but rather ever-changing sets of roles that people take on. Of course, for maximal effectiveness, each role should always fit the skills and strengths of the person filling it, and they should be encouraged to keep developing them even further.

MY PERSONAL PROFILE

In order for everyone in the team to have full clarity about their own and their colleagues' strengths, the next step is to create personal profiles. This happens in a four-step process:

1 Collecting your own strengths

First, write down what you yourself see as your primary strengths. What are you really good at? Where do you make a difference? These can be any aspects that come to mind and don't have to be limited to things beneficial for this particular job. To get another perspective, you can also draw on the answers you received from the people you messaged. And of course, you shouldn't jot down strengths that you disagree with.

2 How your colleagues see you

Now let's expand the viewpoint further by incorporating the views of other team members. Here, we take a piece of paper for each participant and, at the top of it, write the headline: "What I value about [name] is ..." Then, taking turns, each person writes down a few items, and then folds the paper so that their answers are hidden, and only the headline is visible. The paper is passed around the table in this manner until everyone has had a chance to add their thoughts. If people struggle to come up with things to write, it can help to think of concrete situations where the person being evaluated has displayed a strength. This also makes it easier to give concrete examples and context, which is really important—vague strengths like "Smart" or "Reliable" aren't very helpful. At the end of this step, each participant should have something resembling ugly but valuable origami: a piece of paper with lots of folds and creases but plenty of useful information inside.

3 Filling the profiles

Now that everyone has a good view of their strengths, it's time to fill out the profiles of each person. This is done not by the person themselves, but by a partner. So the next step is to pair people up and have everyone listen to their partner and then fill out the template in the image below. The first person should talk for 5—10 minutes, covering the following aspects, based in part on the input they gathered in the previous steps:

- *"What I'm good at is ..."* (Strengths)
- *"Talk to me about ..."* (Interests)
- *"Please don't ..."* (Don'ts)

The other person just listens and fills out the profile with notes. When the pair is done, they reverse roles. And when both profiles are ready, the pair can discuss them if they wish. What's more, if they want, they can add a personal touch to their profile by drawing clothes, facial features, and so forth onto the blank figure in the profile.

NAME

INTERESTS

STRENGHTS

DON'TS

4 Presenting the profiles

The personal profile exercise ends with the whole group sitting in a big circle once again. Each profile is presented to the group, but not by the subject of the profile. Rather, their partner describes them. The idea behind this dynamic is to help people see themselves from someone else's perspective, as well as to help the group build stronger one-on-one connections with no barriers to open communication. And to really get the full benefit here, in step 3, it makes sense to pair up people who may not have the strongest connection yet.

Once all the profiles have been presented, it can be useful to have a brief discussion around them. This enables people to ask for additional details or examples where something is still unclear, as well as providing a space where any missing strengths can be raised. At the end of the discussion, the group must decide what to do with the profiles. Will they be published? If yes, how and by whom?

MY PERSONAL PROFILE

GOAL:
Each participant has a personal profile, capturing their strengths, interests, and don'ts. All profiles have been shared across the group.

4+ PEOPLE

1,5 – 2 HOURS

Post-its, pens, and a flipchart or whiteboard

Distributed authority:
Working with roles and accountabilities

In the last part of the first module, the team learns how to work with roles. This is a key component of the Loop Approach. To understand its importance, let's compare an organization operating based on roles vs. one that relies on traditional jobs. In the workshop, we would ideate these differences together with the team, and we'd probably end up with something like the table below.

JOB	VS.	ROLES
Each job in the company is fixed. When the need arises, the company writes a description for a new job and hires someone for it.		Roles are flexible. They are created and filled as needed, disappearing again when this is no longer the case.
A job is usually a full-time one, intended to take up all the capacity of one person.		A role is precisely and narrowly defined to cover only one specific need of the organization, and it may well only take up a part of a person's time. For example, a valid role in the HR team could be to research recruiting events. Or to ensure the fridge is stacked with beverages.
Salary is typically strongly linked to a person's job, and it's governed by strict rules, at least in most traditional organizations. Changing your job often also means a change in your salary.		Individual roles are often not directly translated into salaries. That's because most employees hold multiple roles at once and are constantly picking up new ones and handing in old ones. This means that new criteria for defining compensation are needed.
In traditional organizations, each employee typically has just one job. There don't tend to be any "accountant/forklift drivers" in most companies. This means that when new jobs need to be filled, new people have to be hired for them.		In a role-based organization, employees can hold multiple roles simultaneously. Each role requires different amounts of time, and the roles each person has might be distributed over several teams. Depending on how the employee prioritizes the roles, the time and energy spent on each can fluctuate from week to week.

Let's look at an example of how these differences manifest themselves. A job-oriented company might have a department head with multiple responsibilities, including some that don't really suit him or her very well. Perhaps they need to calculate the department's profits each month but have absolutely no head for numbers. In a role-based organization, all the department head's responsibilities would be clustered into separate roles, and these roles could be distributed among a team, depending on each person's strengths and preferences. Maybe someone who actually likes crunching numbers should do the profits?

Another split we would typically also recommend would be separating the lead role and the coaching role from each other. This allows the lead role to focus on making strategic decisions, setting goals for the team, and providing performance feedback to team members, while the coach role can focus on developing employees to help them reach their full potential. In a job-oriented company, the department head would need to perform both these functions, even though it's actually quite unusual for one manager to have the necessary skill sets to be successful in both.

If a team has too many roles, things can quickly get confusing. That's why it's important to make explicit all roles and their accountabilities, and to keep this list updated at all times. This gives everyone an easy reference point to check their team's structure. And if, one day, someone leaves the team it'll be easy to see which roles and accountabilities are no longer being fulfilled.

DEVELOPING A FIRST ROLE STRUCTURE

Most of the teams we work with haven't fully embraced roles yet. They are either still organized around jobs, or they've at most implemented roles on a very basic level. That's why we like to go through the following exercise to help each team translate all their relevant work into roles. The exercise only comprises four steps, but before diving in you should know that it can take a fair bit of time.

| Write down all relevant tasks performed

If feasible, it can be a good idea to assign this first step to team members as a preparatory task for the workshop, though this is by no means necessary. In this step, each team member should think about the 5 to 50 recurring tasks that they perform during a typical working week. What we're looking for here are actual tasks, denoted by active verbs, like "Create presentation for sales pitch", "Add customers to CRM system," or "Organize feedback talk with colleague." These should be relevant to the team's work, so items like "Drop the kids off at school" or "Try to read *War and Peace* again" don't belong here. The tasks must also be meaningful and go beyond the things expected of every employee, so not things like "Come to office," "Read emails" or "Type on keyboard to make clickety-clack sounds that contribute to realistic office soundscape."

One way to map out these tasks is for everyone to take a moment at the end of each day over a week and note down what they did during that day, as well as how much time and energy they spent on each task. If they didn't do this as a preparatory task before the workshop, the participants can skim through their calendars and task lists for a bit to try to reconstruct their typical working week.

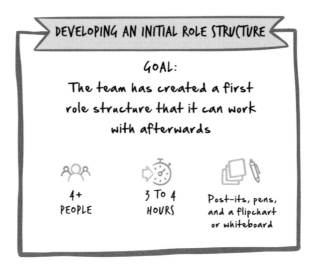

DEVELOPING AN INITIAL ROLE STRUCTURE

GOAL:
The team has created a first role structure that it can work with afterwards

4+ PEOPLE

3 TO 4 HOURS

Post-its, pens, and a flipchart or whiteboard

2 Defining roles and their purpose

In the next step, we take all the tasks we have found and cluster them into roles. To do so, we need a big wall on which people stick post-its, one for each task. Similar tasks or ones that are related to each other can be clustered together. This exercise can either be done individually, or in small groups to encourage peer support.

When a group of tasks belongs under the same broader area of responsibility, they form a role. Once the roles have been demarcated, it's time to add a name and purpose to each one. Here, purpose just means a short description of why the role is needed by the team. This part should be fairly easy as long as each cluster really has a shared denominator that makes sense. If it proves hard to find a name and purpose for a role, it's worth re-examining if the cluster is logical.

Eventually, you should end up with a good understanding of the most important roles that each person has within the team, and indeed, this is what you're aiming for here.

3 Understanding the status quo in roles

Once the most important roles each person holds have been identified, the group as a whole walks along the wall from left to right (or right to left—go nuts), so that everyone gets a brief overview of all the roles in the team. If something isn't clear, there's also room for short discussions and clarifying questions.

Typically, this is a watershed moment for the team: for the first time ever, they have mapped out all their roles, meaning all the areas the team is responsible for. And although no roles have been altered or new accountabilities created yet, it's already very significant that the current reality has been successfully depicted. This is an important step in the journey to embracing a fully role-based approach to work.

4 Making roles explicit

Next, it's time to capture all the roles that were identified. This is done by populating role templates, like the one in the image below, capturing all the key components of each role:

- Each role needs a name, like "Sales closer", "CRM master," or "Feedback guru."
- Each role must also have a clear purpose, depicting an ideal yet unattainable goal, like "Every pitch leads to a sale" or "Our CRM system is always up-to-date."
- Each role has to include a set of accountabilities, meaning recurring tasks like "Updates sales pitch based on feedback," "Suggests new ideas for improving CRM system" or "Collects data from new leads and add them to CRM system."

5 The evolution of the role structure

In this final step, the team takes its first steps in developing and adjusting its role structure, aided by a facilitator. Some questions that the team should answer in this stage include: Of the current roles, which ones are really needed for the team's purpose? Are there any roles missing? What tensions arise looking at the current role structure?

Depending on the tensions raised at this point, new roles may be added. Typically, as the facilitators, we will bring up a few tensions ourselves too. These stem from a short list of standard roles that we believe are important for any team, which is why we propose them unless they exist already:

○ Lead role

The Lead role is responsible for alignment in the team, especially for setting goals, tracking them and coming up with short-term strategies for attaining them. This is a big picture role that gives team members a rough frame to navigate in. Importantly, it's not a classic "predict and control" managerial role that works mainly in short timeframes.

○ Coach role

The Coach role is responsible for developing the people in the team. This role ensures that everyone regularly takes the time to check in with themselves and answer the following questions: "Am I currently effective in my roles? What should I change to become even more effective? Are there any developmental goals I want to set for myself?"

○ Transparency role

This role is responsible for ensuring that all relevant information is always accessible to everyone in the team. The Transparency role also ensures that all documentation is comprehensive and up-to-date. As you can see, this is yet another responsibility that is typically wrapped into a manager's job, but here, we're able to split it off into its own role.

○ Facilitator role

The Facilitator role is responsible for ensuring that all meetings are effective and participants abide by the rules. This role is only active during meetings, and unlike the roles above, it can also be rotated from one meeting to the next, as long as whoever performs it is competent to do so.

○ Loop Ninja

The Loop Ninja role is responsible for maintaining a smooth Loop process. Typically, this role starts their work immediately by ensuring that all the next steps agreed on in the workshops get tracked and done afterwards.

ROLE

CIRCLE

PURPOSE

Is responsible for...

ACCOUNTABILITIES

This is the end of Module 1. Ideally, all the goals defined at the beginning of the module can now be checked off. If not, then guess what: we've got ourselves another tension. It can be discussed and resolved right away, or in the next module. But to recap, what we said we'd need to see to consider this module a success was that...

- ☑ the team has understood what the Loop Approach is and what its building blocks are,
- ☑ the team has defined and documented its purpose, as well as goals for the near and mid-term future,
- ☑ the strengths and potential of each team member have been identified and made transparent throughout the team. And in the process, the team members have gotten to know each other a little better and formed stronger connections,
- ☑ each team member knows their areas of responsibility in the team and has packaged them into roles. Those roles have been made transparent and are clearly distinct from one another,
- ☑ the team has understood the concept of tensions and started applying it to their daily work.

AGENDA MODULE 1 (EXAMPLE)
– DAY 1 –

9⁰⁰   Check-in

9³⁰   Context & Mindset

10¹⁵   Input: Working with tensions

10⁴⁵   Coffee break

11⁰⁰   The 7 Habits: taking stock

12⁰⁰   Introduction to Purpose

12³⁰   Lunch break

13³⁰   Warm-up

13⁴⁵   Purpose playoffs

15⁴⁵   Coffee break

16⁰⁰   People profiles

16⁴⁵   Processing tensions

17³⁰   Check-out

AGENDA MODULE 1   (EXAMPLE)
– DAY 2 –

9^{00} Check-in

9^{30} Recap day 1

10^{00} Review purpose

10^{30} Coffee break

10^{45} Input on roles

11^{00} Working with roles

12^{30} Lunch break

13^{30} Warm-up

13^{45} Cont. with roles

15^{45} Coffee break

16^{00} Tensions and next actions

16^{45} Check-out

*T*he first goal of Module 2 is to ensure that the results from Module 1 get implemented in the team's everyday work. In a typical team transformation, we'd first wait a few weeks after Module 1 so that the team has a bit of time to integrate and test their new behaviors and practices in real life. Then, Module 2 starts and we ask: "How can we translate this clarity into real results? How can we rev up all our engines and set sail at full speed? "

Module 2 can be broken down into two major parts, both of which have to do with the question of how a team can best translate its members' potential and intentions into results. These two parts are:

4 ***Personal effectiveness:*** How can each team member be effective in their own roles and self-organize their work?

5   ***Team effectiveness:*** How can the team comprehensively align on its work, and how should meetings and tools be used for maximal effectiveness?

What we'd need to see in order to consider Module 2 a success is that ...

☐ we've ensured that the outcomes from Module 1 have been translated into the everyday work of the team,

☐ each team member has challenged their own way of self-organizing their work and has discovered some tools they could use to improve further,

☐ everyone in the team knows how to best resolve their own tensions within the team,

- the team has reflected on and adapted their meeting routines. The new routines have been agreed upon together and will be implemented in the team's weekly schedule, right after the workshop is over,
- the team has learned about and adopted new ways of making decisions,
- the workshop has resulted in real improvements to the way the team works together, providing outcomes that can be implemented immediately.

Personal Effectiveness:
How can each of us be effective in our roles?

In the first part of Module 2, we examine how individuals in the team organize themselves. We try to find out how they can keep an overview of their many roles, tasks and projects.

GETTING THINGS DONE

If a team wants to work effectively together, the starting point is individual effectiveness. Here, we ask if each team member has the skills and tools to effectively manage themselves, so that they can fill multiple roles at the same time. This kind of self-management isn't always easy, and the danger with multiple roles is that people fall into a purely reactive mindset, focusing exclusively on dealing with the never-ending stream of inbound tasks and requests. To avoid this, we use the mantra that *you* should decide what work to do—the work shouldn't decide for you.

This is the point in the workshop where we typically give a brief introduction to David Allen's Getting Things Done (GTD) methodology. We're huge fans of it and believe it contains everything needed for good self-management. Depending on the current tensions in the team, we might dive deeper into GTD or also explore other tools here too. But most of the time, presenting the key elements of GTD already provides a strong basis for self-management, as well as for cooperation in the team, thanks to everyone sharing the same approach to structuring and talking about work.

What GTD promises is space and focus. It delivers on this promise by enabling you to get rid of all the loose ends you try and fail to keep organized in your head. Of course, adopting GTD or any similar method requires you to invest a bit of time into organizing your own work, but the upshot is that the work itself will take far less time thanks to your priorities becoming very clear. As David Allen says, the goal of GTD is achieving "stress-free productivity", meaning that you can stay productive and in control even in the face of an an overwhelming amount of things to do. This is possible by defining a specific place for any and all information you come across and using a clear, trusted process for dealing with it.

Let's now take a look at a few of the key ideas we usually discuss in the workshop at this point.

AN INBOX FOR EVERYTHING

The starting point of GTD is that you should use one distinct inbox as a place for collecting all incoming requests for your attention. At this point, these requests aren't yet to-dos or projects—or anything for that matter. All you do here is just collect them, safe in the knowledge that they will be reviewed later on when the inbox is emptied.

To avoid confusion, your inbox in the GTD sense does not mean your email inbox. That's because requests come in through a variety of channels besides email, including phone calls, meetings, and even in the form of ideas you have yourself. Having one inbox to capture all of these is profoundly powerful, and it can take almost any form you wish, from a piece of paper to a digital list on your phone.

In the next step of the GTD flow, you empty your inbox. This means looking at each item and classifying it into one of the following categories:

Irrelevant: Discard it.

Information: Put it somewhere where you can find it again when you need it.

Events: Anything that needs to happen at a specific point in time, like a meeting or an appointment with your doctor. These should go into your calendar.

Actionable items: This is where things get a bit more complicated, so we'll jump out of this bulleted list here and describe what happens to these in the following paragraphs.

For actionable items, the first order of business is to apply the handy two-minute rule introduced in GTD: for everything that you can do in around two minutes or less, just go ahead and do it. The time needed to process items further in the GTD system is just not worth it, and it's easier just to get them out of the way.

Meanwhile, for any item that would take over 2 minutes to complete, you decide whether it's a task or a project. This difference is important and helpful, which is why we encourage teams to adhere to this nomenclature strictly.

A task is a single step that takes no longer than 30—60 minutes to complete. It should be so clearly defined that it takes no mental effort at all to get started. This means that things like "Recruit intern," "Write thesis," or "Solve global warming" don't fall under this category, because they all require significant work just to figure out what tasks are within those broad topics. And please note that all of these criteria also apply to next actions, which are relevant for projects.

A project is a larger undertaking that contains more than one step. It has a clearly defined outcome and at least one next action attached to it. So "Recruit intern" might be a project, and "Set up kick-off meeting with HR" could be the next action attached to it. In complex environments, thinking in terms of next actions is often very helpful. We might not yet know what all the next actions in a given project are, but we do know the ultimate desired result, and we can, at any point in time, define the most sensible next action to get a little closer to it. For this to work, it's important to take the time to make the result of the project crystal clear, as well as to keep it updated, since the goal can change over time as new information becomes available. To help define this result, it's helpful to ask yourself: What's your exact definition of "done"? What will the world look like when the project has been completed?

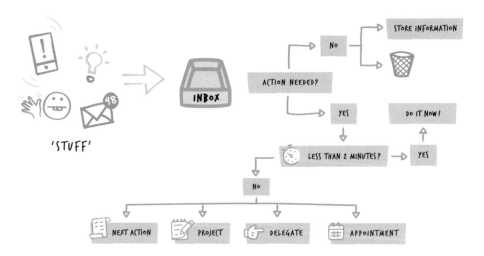

In line with GTD, we typically advise teams to think of projects as something that can be completed in a few weeks or a few months. If something takes years to complete, it should be broken down into multiple, shorter-term projects.

The key to defining descriptive, useful results for projects is to keep asking yourself "What will the world look like when the project has been completed? What's my Definition of Done (DoD)?" Do this, and you'll no longer have vaguely named projects like "Website" or "Build website," but rather something like "The first version of the website is online and can be tested." Such differences in wording might sound trivial at first, but they're actually very impactful. Names like these provide a clear focus for the person working on the project and are instantaneously understandable by anyone who sees them.

What's more, they help avoid the pitfalls of vaguely named projects. Chief among them is the fact that a project like "Build website" can probably never truly be completed. Is it "built" when the first page is up? Hardly. Is it "built" when the whole site is up, but in the meantime ten new ideas and feature requests have come up that also need to be implemented? Hard to say. This ambiguity means that it's never really clear when the website is finally "built" and the project done. "The first version of website is online and can be tested" is much clearer, and it'll be obvious to anyone in the organization when it's done. An additional project around the website may still be needed afterwards, but at least it's clear that this result was delivered.

Another benefit of clearly defined end results is that they help pick and prioritize the right next actions during the projects. The person working on the project can also ask whether a certain next action is the most sensible way of

PROJECTS AND THEIR 'DEFINITION OF DONE'

GOAL:
Participants can distinguis between projects and next actions, and they can verbalize their projects as desired outcomes

1+
PERSON

15
MINUTES

Post-its, pens, and a flipchart or whiteboard

moving toward the goal. As mentioned before, beyond individual effectiveness, we also see GTD as beneficial for collaboration, because it provides a shared language for work: when I say "project," you know exactly what I mean.

That's why, at this point, we ask each team member to define a few projects that they are currently working on as part of their roles in this team. The resulting list of projects will prove useful in the next part of the module.

Team effectiveness: How can we be effective as a team?

Now it's time to zoom out from the individual perspective to one that encompasses the entire team. First, we go back to the concept of tensions, which is central to our approach, and explore how it can be used to improve any meeting.

WHERE TENSIONS BELONG: THE FOUR SPACES

As mentioned in Module 1, tensions don't have any negative connotations—they're just impulses for change. And to ensure that they get resolved effectively and actually result in meaningful change, each tension needs to have the right space to be resolved in. Different tensions call for different spaces, and we'll spend most of the remainder of the book discussing these spaces.

To be able to define these spaces, the first thing we need is a map that pinpoints which tension belongs where. Here, we usually use the concept of the four spaces, as introduced by HolacracyOne partner Tom Thomison.

The four spaces are:

| The operational space. This is where everyday work happens, including all the operational work like exchanging information, distributing tasks, completing tasks, projects, and so forth. Basically, this space is where we spend most of our hours at work. Tensions that could end up in this space might be:

INDIVIDUAL SPACE

Working on myself

OPERATIVE SPACE

Working in my roles

TRIBE SPACE

Relationships and
interpersonal conflicts

GOVERNANCE SPACE

Changing the structure
of the organization

"I need you to do this for me," "I need information," "I would like to request a bigger project from this role," and so forth.

2 **The governance space.** While the operational space is about working in the organization, the governance space is there for working *on* the organization. This entails things like revising roles, changing structures, and creating rules for the team to play by. Any tensions related to rules or missing roles go here. This is to avoid them cropping up in the operational space, where they could easily derail and dramatically slow down meetings.

3 **The individual space:** This is a space that each individual inhabits by themselves. This is where their self-developmental work happens, which is aimed at growth. Questions arising in this space might be "Why am I so frustrated that my colleague hasn't responded to my email yet?" or "What's really important to me in my work and in my relationships with colleagues?" People

resolve tensions here that only pertain to themselves, though, of course, they can still seek support from others to do so.

4   The tribe space. This space contains all the relationships between team members. That's why any tensions pertaining to interpersonal conflict belong here, like "You left my email unanswered, and this upset me." This is also where tensions aiming for stronger relationships can be resolved, such as "We should have a regular pizza and beer evening together as a team."

As you see in the image above, the left half of the matrix comprises the individual and tribe spaces. As Tom Thomison puts it, this is the "relational" side, because it has to do with people and their relationships. Meanwhile, the operational and governance spaces form the "role-ational" side on the right, meaning it has to do with roles, not people. In this book, Module 2 covers the role-ational side, while Module 3 dives into the relational side.

The differences between these four spaces might seem small, but this framework is actually very powerful. A team just has to distinguish between the four spaces and know how to solve tensions in the right ones.

As an example, let's take a look at a typical tension that might arise in a team. Let's say that person A has some kind of personal beef with person B. We could try to solve this tension in the governance space by creating an intermediary role between the two parties. But obviously, it would be better to address this tension in the tribe space, where the team members' relationships reside. There, we can work on those relationships, for instance by unearthing and addressing the underlying reason for why the relationship has soured.

Unfortunately, only a few organizations actually use this approach. In most of the companies we see, the left half of the matrix doesn't even officially exist. This means that personal conflict seeps into the operational or governance spaces, where it's never resolved. What's worse, it often hinders and harms the work done in those spaces.

EXERCISE: SORTING TENSIONS

In this exercise, we want to ensure that everyone in the team has fully understood the four spaces and can work with them. The goal is to sensitize everyone to tensions in their everyday work so that they can perceive and express them. This happens in three steps:

1 **Collecting tensions.** Everyone in the group takes a few minutes to jot down some tensions they feel pertaining to their work in the team. They do this based on their roles, aiming to create impulses for change. If they need some triggers to get their tension-juices flowing, they can skim their emails, diaries, notes, or to-do lists. Here, it's good to emphasize that a tension can be anything that the person feels should be different to the way it is now. This means it's usually accompanied by some kind of emotional response like excitement, frustration, or a feeling of uncertainty.

2 **Discussing in pairs.** After each participant has made a list of tensions, they sit down with their neighbor to discuss. They read through the lists and try to assign each tension to one of the four spaces. If they've written down their tensions on post-it notes, they can stick them directly onto the matrix to illustrate the results.

3 **Discussing as a group.** Last, each pair briefly shares 2—4 of their examples. They explain which tensions belong where and why, and how they would get resolved there. These examples help create a shared understanding that will prove valuable in the future.

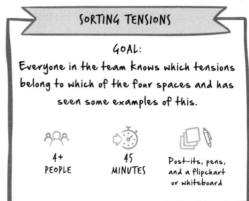

SORTING TENSIONS

GOAL:
Everyone in the team knows which tensions belong to which of the four spaces and has seen some examples of this.

4+
PEOPLE

45
MINUTES

Post-its, pens, and a flipchart or whiteboard

AN ENLIGHTENED APPROACH TO DEALING WITH TENSIONS: "WHAT DO YOU NEED?"

To deal with tensions effectively, the first thing you need to know is which space they belong in. After that, you get to the fun part: solving the tensions. And as we see it, the key to solving them is a small yet powerful question that we first heard about in a Holacracy training session: "What do you need?" It sounds deceptively simple, but when you employ it as a habitual response to tensions, it can be very powerful. (It can also be more than a little annoying, at least initially: "My tension is that you took my chair!"—"What do you need?"—"My chair, you idiot!")

And if you sense a tension, your responsibility doesn't end with merely voicing it in the right space. You are also fully responsible for solving it, and need to figure out what to do. Others can help you do so by asking you the same question as above: "What do you need?"

The typical responses to this question are described in Holacracy as the five pathways:

- I need to share information.
- I need to get information from someone in the team.
- I need someone to take a next action.
- I need a more complex outcome, meaning a project.
- I need a decision regarding a new role or rule.

Examining these five pathways usually makes it very clear to yourself and others what exactly you need to solve your tension.

WORKING IN THE OPERATIONAL SPACE: SYNC MEETINGS

In our experience, the greatest untapped potential for improving a team's work can be found in their meetings. In today's organizations, meetings are where most of the important work and synchronization happens. In fact, most people in most organizations spend most of their time in meetings. That's why it's surprising and a bit disheartening that attendees often tend to see most meetings as fairly unproductive—a waste of time, to varying degrees.

The way we think about it, an effective meeting has two criteria:

- Everyone must know why the meeting is needed—its purpose—as well as why their roles in particular are required to be present.
- A meeting can only be called a success if, as a result, people find themselves more energized to pursue the work they do in the team.

So for us, the next step in the workshop is to boost meeting effectiveness. We do this by evaluating the team's meeting routines and developing new prototypes for improved future meetings. At some point in the module, we typically also present two meeting types that we personally find very effective. These are just templates and can still be adapted as per the team's needs. Both are inspired by Holacracy, and in our experience, they work for around 80% of teams. If this doesn't include yours, feel free to pick different ones.

The first type of meeting we want to introduce is the sync meeting, or tactical meeting, as it's called in Holacracy. Its purpose is to synchronize the work done in the operational space. Topics discussed in sync meetings include: Who's working on which projects, what are the next steps and what information is currently missing? No lengthy discussions or complicated decisions occur in sync meetings, as they belong in separate topic-based meetings. The idea is to ensure that information and work are distributed effectively, which actually also used to be the responsibility of managers.

If you've never been to sync meeting, it will likely impress you. With a good facilitator, it may well be the fastest and most efficient exchange of information you've ever seen. We'll elaborate on the facilitator role later, but for now it's enough for you to know that it's vital for enabling good meetings. In our workshops, we typically first fill this role ourselves but later invite team members to do so, too. This way we can coach them and provide feedback, enabling them to keep facilitating meetings long after we've left.

The standard agenda for a sync meeting looks like this:

1 Check-in. All team members take turns sharing what's on their mind and what has their attention right now. More experienced teams can begin to vary their check-in questions as they deem appropriate.

2 Checklist. A team goes through a checklist comprising any recurring tasks that should be verified as completed on a regular basis. This could include items like "All invoices have been paid," or "The weekly newsletter has been sent." If there aren't any relevant checklist items, the list is left empty.

3 Metrics. This section is meant to ensure that the team has all the relevant data they need. This can include metrics like the number of products sold last week or total social media reach. If a team uses a tool like OKRs (see glossary for more details), they might also be tracked here.

4 Project updates. In line with GTD, the team should capture all relevant project-work in a projects list. In this part of the meeting, this list gets reviewed with questions like: "What's new here since our last meeting?" Please note though that this section isn't about status updates, but about *relevant* updates. A response of "No update" is valid and frequently used.

5 Open agenda. The group has an open agenda—a tension stash—on which tensions are captured before and during the meeting. More items can be added all the way up to the end of the meeting. This leniency is needed because the information shared in the meeting up to this point frequently triggers more tensions, which need to be captured and resolved, too.

6 Processing the agenda. Here, the open agenda is emptied. For each item, the facilitator asks the person who raised it the simple question: "What do you need?" Since this meeting typically lasts less than an hour and the agenda usually contains lots of tensions, it's important to focus on finding next actions quickly and sharing information only briefly. No lengthy discussions should take place here. If they are clearly needed, a next action could be to set up a separate meeting with the relevant stakeholders to have such a discussion. It's the facilitator's responsibility to ensure that all the items on the agenda can be processed in the time available. Meanwhile, the transparency role captures all the next actions and other relevant outputs that arise as the agenda is processed.

7 Check-out. At the end of the meeting, participants take turns to share their reflections on the meeting. This can include improvement ideas for next time as well as any things they feel they need to say to end the meeting well.

We've found this meeting structure to be quite effective, but you should of course feel free to adapt it as you see fit. Just be sure to keep in mind the purpose of this meeting: it should provide a space where the team can synchronize on their work, clear any operational obstacles, such as missing information, and regularly review and define next actions.

At this stage of the workshop, the team splits up into groups of say, four people each. We then task each group with creating their vision of a meeting prototype. Fruitful questions to ask at this point are: "What kind of meeting would best fulfill this purpose for us? What would that meeting look like? When and where would it take place?" Encourage the groups to be as concrete as possible, defining the list of participants, the holders of the facilitator and transparency roles, the meeting cadence, the checklist items and metrics to look at, the way notes will be shared and so forth.

After about 30—45 minutes, the small groups present their prototypes to the whole team. The next challenge is then to integrate the various perspectives. The outcome should be a meeting prototype that's safe enough to try because everyone in the team had the chance to raise tensions and include their perspective. The goal isn't to find the perfect meeting format that can never be improved upon, but rather something that will work for now and can be changed later as tensions arise.

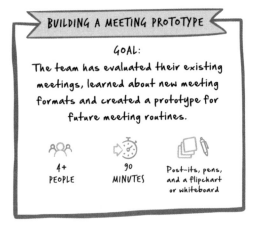

BUILDING A MEETING PROTOTYPE

GOAL:
The team has evaluated their existing meetings, learned about new meeting formats and created a prototype for future meeting routines.

4+
PEOPLE

90
MINUTES

Post-its, pens, and a flipchart or whiteboard

MAKING DECISIONS IN A TEAM

Decision-making in teams is a fascinating topic to explore, partially because it's so often a frustrating and time-consuming process with lacklustre results. That's why one of the goals of the Loop Approach is to clarify exactly how and where decisions are being made in the team. If a decision falls under the responsibility of a role, then obviously it's the role-holder's call. But situations often arise in everyday work where it's not totally clear who can make the decision. In most cases when this happens, we recommend using the consent-method, which we also introduce to the team at this point in the workshop.

In an autocracy, one person decides what to do. In a democracy, the majority decides what to do. In the consensus method, everyone has to agree on what to do. But in the consent method, the best argument determines what to do.

In a democracy and under the consensus-method, we count the "Yes" votes, but with the consent method, we only ask for "Noes." More specifically, we ask for objections to a proposal. In other words, someone makes a proposal and asks if anyone sees a reason why it might cause harm or constitute a step back for the organization. And even if an objection is raised, it doesn't spell the end of the proposal. Rather, all objections are integrated into the proposal, meaning a new, adjusted version is made that takes the objections into account.

So how can a team make real decisions based on consent? Here, we typically present a tool that we've discovered through our work with Holacracy: the Integrative Decision Making process, or IDM for short. You can think of it as a quasi-Design Thinking process that's running on six espressos and some Adderall. IDM comprises the following seven steps:

1 Tension. What's the problem we're trying to solve? Here, the person who brought up the issue describes the underlying tension.

2 Proposal. The person who raised the tension is also responsible for making a first proposal as to how to solve it. If needed, they can ask for help in this.

CONSENT

A NEW WAY OF DECISION-MAKING

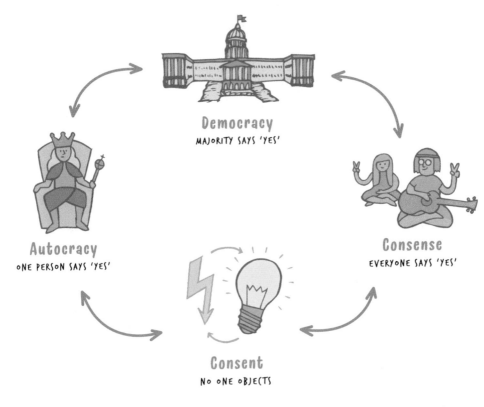

Democracy
MAJORITY SAYS 'YES'

Autocracy
ONE PERSON SAYS 'YES'

Consense
EVERYONE SAYS 'YES'

Consent
NO ONE OBJECTS

#1 Everyone can make a proposal

#2 All objections are considered and tested

#3 All valid objections are integrated

3 Clarifying Questions. If needed, team members can now ask questions to better understand the proposal, and the person who made the proposal can answer them. These can really only be clarifying questions at this point, not reactions masquerading as questions, like "Do you really think this is going to solve anything, you human waste of space?!"

4 Reaction Round. Here, everyone besides the person who made a proposal can provide feedback and share their thoughts. The goal is to help improve the proposal, and the proposer may wish to take notes to manage the flood of information.

5 Amend & Clarify. Once everyone has had a chance to react, the person who made the proposal can respond to these reactions. They can also use any feedback they found useful to change and improve their proposal.

6 Objection Round: Now, one by one, everyone says if they see a reason why the revised proposal from step 5 would cause harm or move the team backwards. But not all of these objections might be valid. A litmus test for the validity of an objection is to ask: "Despite this objection, is the proposal safe enough to try?" If the answer is yes, then the objection is invalid.

7 Integration. Finally, all valid objections are integrated into the proposal. This means that the facilitator asks the person who made the proposal and the person who objected to it to find a new proposal that they are both happy with. This new, improved proposal might have created new objections, so the facilitator goes back to the objection round. Only when all objections have been integrated is the IDM process complete.

In this way, IDM should always eventually lead to a proposal that includes all relevant perspectives and is safe enough to try. This process can also can be used in meetings like the governance meeting that we'll present in Module 3. It can also take the form of the *advice process*, as described by Frederic Laloux

THE ADVICE PROCESS

THE BETTER VERSION OF AUTOCRACY

'Who has the know-how?'

MY TENSION

MY DECISION

MY PROPOSAL

collect opinions and integrate them according to your best judgement

'Who is affected?'

→ Role?
→ Circle?

'Is my role authorized to make this decision?'

Yes → Just do it

No → ~~Boss needs to decide~~ Advice Prozess ↺

in *Reinventing Organizations*. The great benefit of the advice process is that the whole team doesn't need to be in the same room for a decision to get made. Rather, one person translates a tension into a proposal and then identifies stakeholders who are relevant for the proposal, based on their roles and expertise. Then the person seeks feedback from each stakeholder individually or in one big meeting, considering and possibly integrating their views and possible objections. Finally, the decision is made and announced to the team and the stakeholders so that everyone is on the same page.

As before, feel free to be skeptical when it comes to all the tools and principles we presented in this module. If you find ways to adapt and improve them for your own needs, go for it! In any case, we've now covered another important aspect of a team's work: how decisions are made. This brings us to the next module, where we'll examine how a team can keep evolving in terms of roles, rules, and personal relationships to continually become even more effective over time. But before we delve into this topic, let's first see if we can check off the goals we formulated at the beginning of this module. We said we'd consider this module a success if...

- ☑ we've ensured that the outcomes from Module 1 have been translated into the everyday work of the team,
- ☑ each team member has challenged their own way of self-organizing their work and has discovered some tools they could use to improve further,
- ☑ everyone in the team knows how to best resolve their own tensions within the team,
- ☑ the team has reflected upon and adapted their meeting routines. The new routines have been agreed upon together and will be installed in the team's weekly schedule, right after the workshop is over,
- ☑ the team has learned about and adopted new ways to make decisions,
- ☑ the workshop has resulted in real improvements to the way the team works together, providing outcomes that can be implemented immediately.

AGENDA MODULE 2 (EXAMPLE)
– DAY 1 –

9^{00} Check-in

9^{30} Recap Module 1

10^{00} Input: 4 Spaces

10^{45} Coffee break

11^{00} Tensions in 4 Spaces

12^{00} Working with project lists

12^{30} Lunch break

13^{30} Warm-up

13^{45} Input: Sync meeting

14^{00} Exercise: Sync meeting

15^{15} Coffee break

15^{30} Building a meeting prototype

16^{45} Processing tensions

17^{30} Check-out

AGENDA MODULE 2   (EXAMPLE)
– DAY 2 –

9⁰⁰   Check-in

9³⁰   Recap day 1

10⁰⁰   Working with tensions

10³⁰   Coffee break

10⁴⁵   Input on decision-making

11⁰⁰   Practicing IDM

12³⁰   Lunch break

13³⁰   Warm-up

13⁴⁵   Facilitating meetings

15⁴⁵   Coffee break

16⁰⁰   Tensions and next actions

16⁴⁵   Check-out

EVOLUTION

*T*he third and final module of the Loop Approach deals with evolution. We address the question of how a team can continue to solve all the inevitable problems that will arise in the organization, without having to rely on external parties like consultants.

The module has two major building blocks:

6 **High adaptability:** How will our team change its structure when needed? How do we create and change roles and rules within our team?
7 **Conflict & feedback competence:** How do we, as a team, give each other feedback on a regular basis in a way that improves our work and relationships? How can we solve conflicts in a way that fuels our development?

We consider this last module the most important one in the Loop Approach. In order to consider it a success, by the end of it we want to have accomplished the following:

☐ We've ensured that the results from Modules 1 and 2 have been integrated into and are being lived by the team.
☐ The team has a defined governance process, which it uses to continuously change its structure.
☐ The team has practiced using a feedback format and has integrated this format into its meeting routines.
☐ All team members have improved their skills for conflict resolution, enabling them to solve interpersonal tensions more effectively.
☐ We've created a safe space as well as fostered candor and trust between team members, laying a stronger foundation for collaboration.
☐ All remaining questions regarding the Loop Approach have been answered, and the next steps are clear to everyone.

High adaptability:
How will we change the team's structure?

Constant environmental change is an inevitable and ceaseless challenge for every organization today. Therefore it's crucial for an organization to adapt quickly and efficiently to new conditions as they arise. If this is to be accomplished without expensive help from overpaid and overdressed consultants, the teams must learn how to rapidly change its own structure by themselves when needed. This is the topic we'll delve into in the first building block of this module.

WORKING IN THE GOVERNANCE SPACE: THE GOVERNANCE MEETING

After introducing the sync meeting format in the Module 2 workshop, we now present a second powerful meeting: the governance meeting, first introduced as a part of Holacracy. Unlike the sync meeting, which deals with operational issues, the goal of the governance meeting is to work together to develop the team further. It's there so that for once, people can work *on* the organization, not *in* the organization. Complex decisions can be made there together, with issues ranging from creating new roles, adjusting existing ones and establishing or changing rules or policies. Of course, making smart decisions here requires a good decision-making process like IDM, which you may recall from Module 2.

A typical governance meeting will go something like this:

1 Check-in: What's on your mind? What has your attention right now?

2 Administrative concerns: How much time do we have for this meeting? Will we be taking breaks? Does anyone need to leave earlier or hop out for a bit at some point? If yes, how can we account for this in the agenda so that the meeting can still be effective?

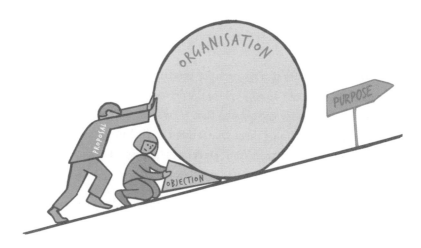

3 Agenda building: In this step, all governance-related tensions are collected from the team. Everyone is encouraged to bring up tensions since they can all potentially help the organization to evolve further. On the agenda, each tension should be described very briefly, using just one or two words, no more.

4 Processing agenda items: Each item on the agenda is processed using the IDM. Each item gets the time it requires, meaning that there may not be sufficient time for all of them to be processed. Therefore, the facilitator might ask the team to prioritize.

5 Check-out: Team members share their reflections on the meeting and say what they feel is necessary in order to leave the meeting on a satisfactory note.

FILLING ROLES IN A GOVERNANCE MEETING

Of course, creating roles in a governance meeting is one thing, but how can you actually fill them? As an example of the process to use, at this point in the workshop, we often raise the tension that we won't be there to facilitate the next meeting. After reviving those who fainted and calming down the hyper-ventilators, we propose that we find someone to fill this role. This can be done through an election, which proceeds as follows:

1   Presenting the role: The person who proposed the role describes what he or she had in mind.

2   Nominations: All participants nominate someone to fill the role. They do so by taking a post-it and writing down the nominee's name as well as their own. Their own name is there so that everyone can see who nominated whom. People can also nominate themselves and are even encouraged to do so when they think the role is right for them.

3   Elaborate on nominations: Everyone explains the rationale for their nominee in turn.

4   Changing nominations: Now that everyone has heard the reasoning behind the various nominations, they can still change theirs.

5   Proposal: The facilitator proposes that the person with the most nominations fills the role. In the event of a draw, the facilitator may propose a candidate by choosing one at random, picking the person who filled the role previously, selecting the person who proposed themselves or asking for nominations again from everyone who didn't propose the candidates who tied.

6   Objection round: The Facilitator asks everyone in the team if they have an objection to the proposal. This includes the person who is being proposed for the role; they can refuse to take it on.

7   Closing: If no objections arise, the role is assigned to the proposed person. A new election can be called at any time if new tensions come up.

And that's how roles can be assigned!

But please remember that just as with the sync meeting, the governance meeting and the election process should be considered prototypes. The team can amend or tweak them as it sees fit. After all, the end goal is for each team to find the meeting routines that work for them. And since meetings take up so much time, it's almost always worth the effort to continue experimenting and evolving the routines further.

Conflict & feedback competence: How can we give each other powerful feedback and resolve conflicts?

In this second part of Module 3, we shift away from the right half of the four space model, meaning the role-ational side of work. Instead, we focus on the relational half on the left that deals with people. For most of us, this is the more difficult half to navigate. While many people in traditional organizations might already have some experience in the role-ational half, the relational half is a complete mystery to them. This is a shame, because dealing with conflict effectively and ensuring regular feedback can be extremely powerful skills to master. On the other hand, this is also what makes those who do master them so valuable.

WE ALL HAVE THE SAME BASIC NEEDS

FOR INSTANCE...

CONNECTION

HUMOR

EFFICACY

NONVIOLENT COMMUNICATION

One of the great benefits of nonviolent communication (NVC) is that it provides a shared language for a team to deal with interpersonal tensions. Though the name may conjure up images of hippies in drum circles, the primary goal here is not to become more peaceful. (Not to say that wouldn't be a worthwhile goal.) Rather, NVC is about communicating in a way that's based on needs. And this method just so happens to be perfectly suited for the way the human brain functions.

NVC is based on two key assumptions: First, people in general would prefer to increase the well-being of others rather than decrease it. Second, all people generally share the same needs. However, they choose very different strategies when it comes to getting those needs fulfilled. And these different strategies give rise to conflict. If, in a conflict situation, a team manages to unearth and talk about the needs underlying the conflict, then it can probably be resolved in a constructive way. "Constructive" here means that the relationships in the team are strengthened by the experience, fostering a more pleasant, trust-based modus of collaboration going forward. The main point of NVC is simply that all people share the same needs, and these needs can always be seen as positive things. You'll find a few examples of this in the image below.

The following images portray two different scenes, and they demonstrate the difference between a conflict occurring on the level of strategies to fulfill needs vs. the actual underlying needs themselves. As you can see, when two people first understand each other's needs, it's usually possible for them to find a win-win solution in terms of strategies, too. And what's more sometimes this can be surprisingly easy!

STRATEGIES & EMPATHY

THERE ARE DIFFERENT STRATEGIES
HOW TO FULFILL THE SAME NEED

WHEN LOOKING AT THE STRATEGIES WE USE,
CONFLICTS OFTEN SEEM LIKE ZERO-SUM GAMES

EMPATHY IS THE KEY TO SOLVING CONFLICTS — IT'S FOCUSSING ON NEEDS.
WHENEVER WE MANAGE TO UNDERSTAND EACH OTHER ON THE LEVEL OF NEEDS,
IT GETS EASY TO FIND A WIN-WIN SOLUTION ON THE LEVEL OF STRATEGIES

THE FOUR ELEMENTS OF EFFECTIVE COMMUNICATION

In order to connect with and better understand others in complicated situations, it's important and helpful to first understand ourselves and our own motives. Here, the four steps of NVC provide a helpful tool to do so in everyday situations.

1 My observation: What is objectively happening? What can you really observe here, putting aside all interpretation from your side? For instance: "I didn't receive an answer from you to my email from the day before yesterday."

2 My feeling: How do you feel about this? What feelings arise in you? For example: "I'm frustrated and angry."

3 My needs: Which needs of yours are affected by this? For instance: "I need to feel respected by others and want to make good use of my time."

4 My request: What would you like to request from the other person? For example: "In the future, would you be willing to try answering emails by the end of the business day?"

Hopefully, it should be pretty easy to see why these four steps are helpful and what purpose they each serve. Unfortunately, implementing them in your day-to-day life is much harder. That's why, in the workshop, we also provide some exercises to help internalize and practice these four steps. These exercises are especially helpful in making some of the key distinctions needed to properly use NVC: separating observations from interpretations, feelings from masked judgments, strategies from needs, and demands from requests.

OBSERVATIONS VS. INTERPRETATIONS

When we observe something, it's human nature to immediately interpret it—this saves us time. When our ancestors saw a sabre-toothed tiger running at them, they were more likely to survive by immediately making the interpretation that they were in danger. But to become more mindful and effective communicators, we need to sever the tie between observation and interpretation. And in order to get the team to reflect on the important distinction between them, at this stage we ask:

Who here has ever seen a messy children's bedroom?

Typically, a few hands will go up. But this raises the question of who gets to decide what a tidy or messy room looks like? What, in fact, can be observed and described about the room without applying a layer of interpretation? And is the interpretation of the room being messy helpful in any way?

An easy way to tell if something is an interpretation is if someone could respond to it with: "That's not true!" Of course, this is the very trait that makes interpretations prime fodder for conflicts that lead nowhere, and only result in hurt feelings, anger and friendship bracelets being tearfully hurled off bridges. But if you stop to think about it, this doesn't really make sense. Time is too precious to spend on arguing about whose interpretation is right. And it's just much easier to communicate based on known facts and concrete observations.

FEELINGS VS. MASKED JUDGMENTS

Feelings occur inside people, and it's important to know them in order to effectively communicate with others. Too often we steamroller our underlying feelings, and jump straight to judging a situation. For example, you might say that you feel ignored by a colleague. But that's not a feeling; it's just your judgment of what your colleague is doing. Real expressions of feelings usually begin with "I am ..." So rather, the real, underlying feeling could be something like: "I am lonely."

This is a fine, delicate distinction, but an important one, because a person can express their own feelings without judging or accusing anyone else. Feelings are very valuable because they are ever-present, and they can be used to provide clarity to a situation without provoking conflict.

We like to clarify the difference between feelings and masked judgments through a mime exercise. Here, participants pick post-its with feelings or masked judgements written on them and try to act them out by miming. The rest of the group tries to guess which feeling or judgment they're trying to convey.

Some examples:

- I am happy
- I am tired
- I am angry
- I am sad
- I feel excluded
- I feel exploited
- I feel manipulated
- I feel trapped

The team typically discovers that it's much easier to act out real feelings than judgments.

NEEDS VS. STRATEGIES

The important difference between these two terms is that strategies are the ways in which we try to get our needs fulfilled. To highlight this distinction in the workshop, we ask each participant to tell us about one thing that they did yesterday as well as the need underlying it. For example, someone might share how they went out for a drink with friends due to their need for social connection. Then, the group collects some of their needs in life and tries to find strategies for fulfilling them. This results in questions like:

- How can I fulfill my need for calm?
- How can I fulfill my need for connection?
- How can I fulfill my need for respect and appreciation?

PRACTICING THE 4 STEPS OF NVC

GOAL:
Everyone in the team knows
the four steps and can find
examples for each

4+
PEOPLE

50
MINUTES

Post-its, pens,
and a flipchart/
whiteboard

REQUEST VS. DEMAND

When we voice demands instead of requests, conflict can easily arise. But it's not always easy to tell them apart. A key difference is that at its core, a request honors the autonomy of the other person, whereas a demand does not. To see which one you're dealing with, it can be helpful to examine a few factors:

- A request always relates to concrete behavior, whereas a demand is often more abstract. So a request could be something like "I would like to ask you to not look at your smartphone during this meeting," whereas a demand would rather be: "Please be more respectful toward the other participants in the meeting."
- A request is generally positive, whereas demands are often phrased negatively. For example, a request might be formulated as "Could you please tell me...," whereas a demand is more likely to be something like "I don't want you to..."
- A request focuses on the present, rather than the past or future: "Would you be willing to tell me now that in the future, you are prepared to..." So even though the behavior involved might only occur in the future, the request itself is always aimed at the present.
- Finally, a request should always allow for the possibility of refusal. A demand often implies that "No" is not an acceptable option, and this severely limits the autonomy of the other person.

GIVING POWERFUL FEEDBACK

So, you might be wondering, why did we present all these communication exercises just now? Because they will help the team in a very important aspect of work: giving feedback. The four steps of NVC allow people to give candid, unsugarcoated feedback in a way that doesn't sting. Given in this way, feedback becomes a gift for everyone involved: the person giving it has a channel through which to express themselves, whereas the person receiving it gets a chance to reflect and develop themselves. Everyone has blind spots, and an outside perspective can be the only way to uncover them and expand one's horizons to encompass them. And hey, no-one's putting a stapler to anyone's head: the person giving feedback is merely offering information— it is up to the recipient whether to use it or not.

Generally, we can distinguish between two kinds of feedback, each of which should play an important part in every working relationship:

- *Situational feedback:* This is the kind of feedback people share continually and informally as relevant situations arise during the day. Typically, this happens whenever they want to express appreciation for something or sense a tension. Think: "Hey, good job on the Fisher deal!" or "I hate it when you steal my stapler." When giving this kind of feedback, the four steps of NVC should be used.
- *Comprehensive feedback:* This is the kind of feedback people give each other periodically. It requires time, a safe space, and a clearly-defined format. Ideally, it should happen in a moderated session. The goal of these sessions is to help the team learn and grow together.

TWO KINDS OF FEEDBACK

FEEDBACK IS IMPORTANT FOR ANY TEAM,
ESPECIALLY SELF-ORGANIZED ONES

SITUATIONAL

⚡ ad hoc

⊙ situational

⏱ prompt

👥 1:1

e.g. after a shared
experience

COMPREHENSIVE

📅 at fixed intervals

🔄 overarching

🔍 retrospective

👥 in the group

e.g. hot seat,
retrospective

→ A proven format, useful for both cases:

I LIKE: ...
I WISH: ...

- start with appreciation

- constructive feedback,
  using "I" messages

SITUATIONAL FEEDBACK: SPEEDDATING

The team can practice giving situational feedback with a small exercise. To prepare, they form pairs that will change throughout the exercise. In each pair, the partners give feedback to each other using the following format:

1. Three minutes of silence during which both partners can take notes to prepare their feedback.
2. Person A gives three minutes of feedback to person B.
3. Person B gives feedback to person A.
4. Both partners discuss and reflect on the feedback they received.

After the discussion, everyone finds a new partner and the process is repeated. It's important that when feedback is being given, the recipient just listens. Step 4 is dedicated to discussion. And if people are struggling to come up with good feedback, it can be helpful to pose the following questions:

○ *What has your partner done recently that you liked a lot?*
○ *What has your partner done recently that irritated you, and how might they behave differently in the future?*

FEEDBACK SPEED DATING

GOAL:
The participants have practiced giving feedback to each other, based on the 4 steps of effective communication

4+
PEOPLE

45
MINUTES

Post-its, pens, and a flipchart or whiteboard

Tips for good Feedback

Impulse
Feedback is only useful when the other person is open to it.

Observation
Describe the situation as precisely as possible. General or vague descriptions often cause confusion or resistance in the other person.

Feelings
The basis of your feelings lies in your own needs and values.
Other people's actions or words are just a trigger. Own your feelings.

Needs
Every person chooses freely which needs or values are of particular importance for her*him in a specific situation. Don't make the claim that you are universally and absolutely right.

Request
What happened is over. Backwards-oriented requests can not be fulfilled and therefore tend to cause resistance in the other person. Pay attention to being solution-oriented and looking into the future when making requests.

Dialogue
The point is to understand each other's perceptions of specific situations and behaviors and not to start a debate in which someone 'is right'.

BUILDING A FEEDBACK ROUTINE

We've now covered situational feedback, but you'll recall that the team also needs a way to give comprehensive feedback, which is deeper in nature. This requires the team to form a new routine. To help instill it, we like to use a simple exercise that we usually also recommend the team adopt permanently.

It doesn't require much in the way of preparation, but it should be facilitated by someone capable, and it's often a good idea to ask someone to take notes. This is useful because it enables the person receiving the feedback to focus on it fully, without having to worry about scribbling down the learnings.

The exercise proceeds as follows:

1. The team forms a circle, leaving a small gap for an empty chair. This is "the hot seat," where the person receiving feedback will sit.

2. Ask one person from the team to volunteer to receive feedback from the group as well as another person to take notes.

3. All team members get 1—2 minutes to prepare feedback for the person now sweating profusely in the hot seat. The feedback can follow a simple format like "I like..." or "I wish..." Helpful questions to come up with feedback can be: "What do I like about working with this person?" or "What would I wish from this person for our work together in the future?"

4. Taking turns, everyone in the circle gives their feedback to the person in the hot seat. When it's the note-taker's turn, someone else should take notes.

5. After the round, the person in the hot seat briefly thanks the group for the feedback. He or she may also briefly comment on the feedback received, but this is not required. The person then leaves the hot seat, and the note-taker shares the notes taken.

6. Then, the next person takes the hot seat, no doubt shocked by how quickly the tables have turned on them!

Please note when planning this exercise that its duration increases exponentially in relation to the size of the group. That's because both the amount of feedback to be given and the number of turns in the hot seat both double. So if a group of ten people needs an hour for the exercise, then a group of 20 will need four hours.[5]

After the exercise, the team can reflect on the meeting routines that they built before. Is another standard meeting required to give comprehensive feedback? What benefits could they get from instilling another meeting routine solely for this purpose? Whatever routine they opt for, it's probably best not to hold these comprehensive feedback meetings too frequently, so that people have time to reflect on and put to use the feedback they receive. What's more, it may be best to hold these meetings offsite, away from the everyday work environment, as otherwise people will be too distracted by their day-to-day worries. And again, we typically recommend that they use the hot seat-exercise as the format for these meetings.

THE HOT SEAT

GOAL:
The participants have learned a new format that they can use to give feedback to each other within the group

4+ PEOPLE   30 – 45 MINUTES   Post-its, and pens

---

5 | This is one of several reasons why we usually recommend to think of teams as rather smaller entities: in our opinion, 20 people aren't a team, they're an amalgam of several teams.

SOLVING CONFLICT CONSTRUCTIVELY: THE CLEAR THE AIR-MEETING [6]

Just to recap: The sync meeting is meant for processing all operational tensions. The governance meeting solves tensions relating to the team's structure or roles through the use of decision-making processes like the IDM. Meanwhile, the feedback meeting fuels progress in the individual space. So with three of the four spaces covered, we still need a meeting for the tribe space. This is where the Clear the Air- or CTA-meeting comes in. The goal of this meeting is to provide a safe space where the team can process potentially incendiary feelings like anger, frustration and irritation. It also allows the team to solve any other tensions that affect the tribe space. Besides the sync, governance and feedback meetings, this is the fourth standard meeting format we typically recommend that most teams adopt.

You'll find the structure for the CTA meeting below, but please note that to truly make it effective, someone should facilitate it—ideally someone who has had NVC training. [7]

1 Check-in: The meeting starts with a *deep check-in*. Sitting in a circle, each person is asked: "What have you celebrated recently? What have you regretted?" The answers need not necessarily be limited to work only: if participants feel comfortable sharing something personal, they may also do so.

2 Collecting interpersonal tensions: Next, everyone takes turns presenting their interpersonal tensions, jotting them down on a whiteboard. For each tension, they also write their own name, the intensity of the tension on a scale from 1 to 10 and the number of people involved in the tension besides the person bringing it up. At this point, those involved are not yet named.

---

6   This meeting was introduced to us by Georg Tarne. He originally implemented it at his company Soulbottles as a "personal relations meeting" and later published it as the Clear the Air-meeting.

7   Warning: While this meeting type can greatly improve relationships in a team, we really only recommend it if facilitated by a seasoned NVC coach. Otherwise, it may do more harm than good.

3 Processing tensions using the mirror method: Next, all the tensions are processed one by one, starting with the weakest tension, meaning the one with the lowest intensity score. Person A explains his or her tension and the person affected (person B) just listens. Then person B attempts to mirror back what they heard, without commenting on it or applying their own perspective in any way. Only after person A has verified that person B has fully understood the tension can person B respond with his or her own perspective. Then, person A mirrors what they've heard back to person B, until person B confirms that they've been understood. This discussion continues back-and-forth until person A feels that their tension has been properly understood. It's the facilitator's main job to ensure that this happens. If the tension involves several people, either those affected can select one person to act as their representative, or the above back-and-forth process must happen with everyone involved. Person A must decide which of these options meets their need.

4 Appreciation round: Once all the tensions have been resolved, everyone in the circle gets a turn to answer two questions: "What has someone in this team done for which I'm grateful? What's something that I've learned to appreciate in a team member in the course of working together?"

5 Check-out: At the end of the meeting, all participants check out, expressing whatever they need in order to end the meeting well and allow the team to move on.

Tips for the Clear-The-Air-Meeting

Before collecting tensions, a moment of silent reflection can be helpful.

The facilitator helps the parties to convey their message and be heard. The focus is on understanding the other party's positive intention and the needs behind the behavior.

"Mirroring" is an important part of successful communication in conflict situations. Experienced participants can often reflect the essential message in just a few words. Whenever a *need* is mentioned, it is important to mirror it.

The facilitator can provide symbols for "sender" and "receiver" and give them to the respective parties when processing tensions. This clarifies the roles in the conversation.

While processing conflicts the focus is on the person who first reported the tension (the sender) and the receiver. Often, several people want to comment on the conflict, but they are not the primary focus. There is room for their opinions and comments as soon as there is a sense of conflict resolution between sender and receiver and the sender, when asked, "What do you need?" feels ready to listen to suggestions from the others. Mirroring should be used here as well.

ITERATING ON THE MEETING ROUTINES

By the time we get to the end of Module 3 in the workshop, the team should have a strong basis from which to start examining if they need to supplement their current meeting routines somehow. Would any of the insights or new meeting formats introduced here be valuable for them? Useful questions to ask include: How can they ensure that there's a governance space for continually working on the structure of the team[8]? How can they resolve conflict and give each other feedback in an effective and constructive way?

To get started, the team first reflects on what's already there: what meetings do they currently use, what new tensions relate to them and how can they be resolved? Then, as the very last exercise of this module, the team splits into two groups, each of which comes up with a prototype for new, adapted meeting routines. Then, both of these prototypes are integrated into a single version, which should include information about all the team's regular meetings, their purpose, and participants. What's more, the frequency of each meeting type should be defined: some may be needed every week, like sync meetings, whereas for others a monthly or quarterly interval may suffice. As the last step of the exercise, the team must define the concrete next steps needed to bring these new meeting routines into their everyday work.

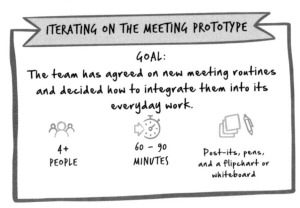

ITERATING ON THE MEETING PROTOTYPE

GOAL:
The team has agreed on new meeting routines and decided how to integrate them into its everyday work.

4+
PEOPLE

60 – 90
MINUTES

Post-its, pens, and a flipchart or whiteboard

---

8   Besides the governance meeting format presented here, governance discussions can also be had in a less formalized way. For many teams, regular retrospective meetings are a good starting point for fostering shared reflection and learning.

Last but not least in the workshop, we take a bit of time to reflect on where the team began its journey, comparing that prior state to where it now stands. Ideally, the following goals that we defined in the beginning of the module can now be checked off:

☑ We've ensured that the results from Modules 1 and 2 have been integrated into and are being lived by the team.

☑ The team has a defined governance process, which it uses to continuously change its structure.

☑ The team has practiced using a feedback format and has integrated this format into its meeting routines.

☑ All team members have improved their skills for conflict resolution, enabling them to solve interpersonal tensions more effectively.

☑ We've created a safe space as well as fostering candor and trust between team members, laying a stronger foundation for collaboration.

☑ All remaining questions regarding the Loop Approach have been answered and the next steps are clear to everyone.

AGENDA MODULE 3 (EXAMPLE)
– DAY 1 –

9^{00} Check-in

9^{30} Recap Module 1 & 2

10^{00} Input: Nonviolent communication

10^{45} Coffee break

11^{00} Practicing 4 NVC steps

12^{30} Lunch break

13^{30} Warm-up

13^{45} Input: Feedback

14^{00} Exercise: Feedback speed dating

15^{15} Coffee break

15^{30} Exercise: Hot seat

16^{45} Processing tensions

17^{30} Check-out

AGENDA MODULE 3   (EXAMPLE)
– DAY 2 –

9:00	Check-in
9:30	Recap day 1
10:00	Input: governance
10:30	Coffee break
10:45	Governance meeting
11:00	Practicing IDM
12:30	Lunch break
13:30	Warm-up
13:45	Input: Conflict
14:00	Exercise: CTA meeting
15:00	Coffee break
15:15	Reviewing meeting prototype
16:00	Tensions and next actions
16:45	Check-out

A Loop comprises three workshop modules, each of which requires about two days to cover. The modules build on one another, following the three steps of the Loop: Clarity, Results, Evolution.

By undergoing these three modules, a team will change all relevant aspects of its work and learn how to translate the Loop Mindset into its everyday behaviors.

At the end of a Loop, the team can continue its journey because it now understands all key aspects of self-organized work and how to work with tensions to improve further.

THE BROADER TRANSFORMATION ARCHITECTURE

*T*he Loop Approach never really ends, because any team that transforms itself through it will continue looping and improving indefinitely. The first Loop is over once the team has finished the three modules, but the transformation itself doesn't stop here. In fact, this is merely the beginning: the team has learned how to make meaningful changes in all aspects of its work, meaning that it now possesses: the most powerful tools needed to bring about a broader transformation in the organization, working from the inside out.

We firmly believe that any successful transformation needs to proceed as a team-based change program. Even the largest organization can be broken down into teams, and you've just learned how to change those. However, we understand that especially in larger organizations, a broader transformation project still requires something more: all the planning and steering that happens around the work within the teams. This is important in order to support the Loops with the right initiatives.

Again, since we're no longer in the old predict-and-control mindset, we can't provide a precise blueprint for this, because we don't know exactly what it will look like for every organization. But we do want to help you apply our most relevant learnings and implement the right workstreams for your transformation. That's why, in this chapter, we'll show you:

- What the right prerequisites and success factors for a broader transformation are.
- What the most important workstreams in the transformation project will be.

When exactly can we say that a transformation has been successful? This question is hard to answer, because success is often a very subjective measure, and change processes are notoriously complex and unpredictable beasts. Nevertheless, we can greatly improve the likelihood of success by ensuring that the basic conditions for it are as good as they can be. This means removing whatever obstacles we can and plotting a course that's similar to previous, successful transformation projects. And to help you do so, we will next present eleven success factors for transformation projects that we've found through our own work.

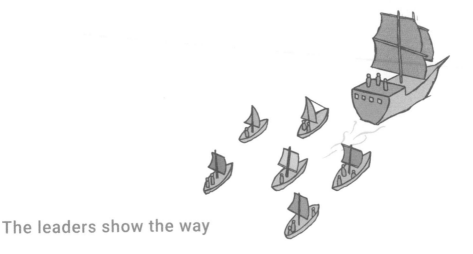

The leaders show the way

In our experience, any transformation is doomed to fail if the leaders in the organization don't fully support it. The people with the power to begin or terminate the transformation need to give their clear commitment to it. In other words...

- the top brass have to see and understand the need for the transformation,
- they have to clearly communicate the need for and their commitment to it,
- they must take the time to fully understand what is happening in the transformation at any given moment,
- they need to lead by example and stick to the new rules that the transformation aims to instill.

The leaders in an organization are often pressed for time, so they can be slow to understand and learn the new behaviors resulting from the transformation. This means that what we often see is leaders communicating a willingness to change but then failing to actually adopt the new behaviors, even sometimes questioning or ridiculing those who have. Imagine, for example, that all teams in an organization have completed Module 2 of the Loop Approach, only to have a senior leader express frustration about all of them using jargon like "tensions" all of a sudden. Obviously, this would be unlikely to help further the transformation, and it's why every leader with the power to help or hinder the transformation needs special attention.

Creating islands of success within the organization

Sometimes it can be hard to convince the executive-level of a larger organization to start a transformation project. In this case, the best strategy is often first to find and transform smaller "islands." These are teams or units that are willing to boldly dive into something new. As the name implies, these islands must be somewhat insular, meaning autonomous enough to try new things and make meaningful changes by themselves. This way, the people on the island can embrace the new tools and methods while being supported by their leadership. As their little transformation advances, the team will start talking about it and the positive impact they have felt. Sooner or later, other teams or units will become interested and want to follow suit. Other leaders around the organization will get curious and decide to create their own islands, too. Eventually, even the top leaders in the organization will want to know more, no matter how sceptical they were initially. And that's when the entire organization can be transformed.

Communicating clear reasons for the transformation

A transformation can succeed if everyone in the organization understands what problems it's meant to solve. To put it in Simon Sinek's terms, the organization needs a shared understanding of the *why* before it can properly being to discuss the *how*. The reason for this is that the transformation will require a lot of hard work, with some setbacks virtually guaranteed. In order to deal with them, a strong shared motivation is needed. Too often organizations merely define the painpoints of the organization, using negatively slanted phrases like "We're too slow" or "We can't currently tap into our full collective potential." But they should also take the time to paint a positive image of the future. How will the world and their work together look like when the transformation is successfully underway? For example: "We can respond to external changes quickly" or "We can put our full potential to use in our roles."

Welcoming all leaders aboard

Even if the top management in an organization is fully committed to the transformation project, it's still entirely possible to encounter resistance. Typically, it arises on the second or third leadership tier in the organization, where people have invested a lot of time and energy to learn how to play the game of politics and as a result have obtained certain powers and privileges that they are reluctant to give up. Will the Executive Jacuzzi Room still maintain its allure once it's the Everyone Jacuzzi Room? These people probably won't openly oppose the transformation as this would carry political risk, but will rather find other ways to sabotage it. To avoid this, it's important to ask questions like:

- How can we get everyone with influence on board?
- What alternative routes to success and privileges can we offer to those who will lose some of their power?
- What career development paths can we offer people in the future?
- How can we start and maintain a dialog with the leaders who are afraid of or oppose the transformation?

Usually, it's worth treating these reluctant leaders with appreciation and empathy. If their opposition can be turned into support, they will become powerful allies that can greatly help the transformation along.

Accept that not everyone will join the journey

No matter how hard you try, there will always be some people who can never be won over to embrace the transformation. This is unavoidable, but fortunately not problematic. In every large organization, it's inevitable that some members don't share all of the organization's values. Of course, this may not be evident yet, because they don't tend to talk about it, and rather just accept their tensions as a given. But in the transformation, our goal is to make it clear to everyone what kind of behavior is and isn't desirable in the organization. This transparency enables every employee to compare their own values and expectations around work to those of the organization. People who sense a misalignment should leave, and the resulting minor exodus is part of a healthy transformation process. As an example, consider Zappos' transformation effort: to ensure that all remaining employees would be onboard, it told them that they could each receive the equivalent of a few months' salary as a bonus if they were to leave.

Find and support strong internal change agents

In any transformation, external consultants can only ever provide impulses for action, but the actual transformation has to happen from within the organization. This requires strong internal change agents who take responsibility for driving the transformation. Ideally, these should be people who understand the Loop Approach or at least are willing to learn it. In addition to this competence, the change agents should ideally also hold leadership positions so that they can use their power to advocate for the transformation. In order to convince leaders to take on this role, it can be helpful to explain that organizational development will be a key aspect of leadership in the future. They should then take the hint that taking on a big role in the transformation could be a wise career move.

Unfortunately, it's not unusual at the beginning of a transformation project that no one wants to take responsibility for it. When asked for resources, leaders tend first to send in a loveable ragtag bunch of people with no real power, or maybe even troublemakers. Unfortunately, this doesn't really provide a solid foundation for the project. Instead, what's needed is a strong internal transformation team that takes full responsibility for the project. And if this team includes leaders from the second leadership tier, it will typically make the transformation more effective and faster.

Communicate continuously

Good communication is a key aspect of successful transformation. It's also hard to ignore, because when a transformation is occurring, employees will typically hound you for more transparency and the opportunity to participate. This is especially true if the changes impact something important to them, like the way their work is defined. Hence, the golden rule of transformation is that it's not really even possible to over-communicate about it. (Well, maybe don't go knocking on people's doors in the middle of the night to tell them about it, but you get the idea.)

Perhaps the most important aspect here is for the top leadership to regularly communicate the current state of the transformation. This means sharing success stories, but also having an open, honest dialog about the challenges. And rest assured, there will be challenges. After the initial excitement has died down, problems and setbacks will inevitably emerge. Nothing blunts people's enthusiasm like no-one having ordered more toilet paper this week due to a role reshuffling.

It will be much easier to deal with these setbacks if they are treated as tensions, meaning opportunities to learn and improve, rather than trying to sweep them under the rug. To do so, it can be a good idea to create spaces where all employees can ask questions about the transformation. This could be as simple as holding discussion sessions where the organization's leadership and change agents invite everyone to attend and talk. Just the act of offering such a forum usually goes a long way in soothing the opposition's concerns, even if they don't actually show up at the session.

Don't expect miracles

"Don't worry, in three months, we'll be completely agile." That's all too easy to say, and unfortunately, there are even some people who are suckered in by such sweet talk. But promises like this create unrealistic expectations that can't be delivered on, resulting in apparent "failures" that can make the whole transformation project look bad.

Happily, it's easy to avoid this dynamic by communicating from the the start that the transformation is going to be a marathon, not a sprint. It'll take a long time and will never be truly over, because the whole point is that the organization must continue to evolve. What's more, often it won't result in any visible improvements in the near future. As one entrepreneur told us when starting to transform his generations-old organization comprising hundreds of people, he only expected to see actual improvements after about three years. Until then, he was willing to accept losses in terms of productivity, morale, and cash-flow due to the time needed to train and reskill employees.

But happily, you don't need to brace yourself for anything that dramatic. The Loop Approach should make transformations much less costly by proceeding so gradually that productivity is not disrupted. But nevertheless, expecting and promising miracles will inevitably result in disappointment.

Focus on pioneers and internal multiplicators

Pioneers are needed in the beginning of every transformation. These are people and teams who are willing to dive into the transformation head first, even if it's not yet totally clear what the impact and working modus will be. The uncertainty they face stems from the fact that the Loop Approach is just a prototype, and it needs to be adapted to the needs of the organization during the process. The first Loops and workshops will inevitably be a bit rocky for the pioneers, but they will smooth the way for those that follow. This is why the pioneers and their teams should have an early adopter mindset, more interested in getting started and experimenting with something new than in having the perfect experience already. This means they need to be carefully picked to find the best possible teams to start the transformation with. Just remember: pioneers should always be volunteers, and they deserve praise for boldly forging a path where there was none before.

The team makes all the difference

We define a team as a group of people who work toward a shared goal and are motivated to do so. The Loop Approach has been designed for such teams, and it may not work well for other groups outside of this definition, for instance if they don't work together or don't pursue shared goals. What's more, the Loop Approach hasn't been designed to fix problematic teams that are, say, in the throes of conflict, about to disband, or that have grown so large and bloated that members barely know each other. That's not to say that such teams can't be helped and transformed, it's just worth keeping in mind that this is not what we specifically created the Loop Approach for. We created it for actual *teams* as per our definition.

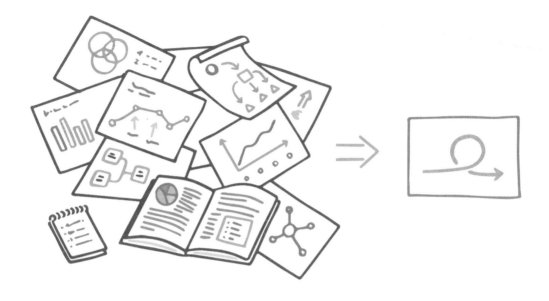

Going beyond change management

The antiquated notion of change proceeding linearly from a clearly defined beginning to a clearly defined end is no longer useful for anyone, and yet is is still at the heart of classical change management. This kind of thinking is based on the old predict-and-control paradigm that the Loop Approach aims to overcome. That's why we're trying to avoid the term *change* as much as possible, and instead replace it with *transformation*, which we hope is free from the burden of these old connotations. We believe that a transformation can only be successful if the process itself reflects and broadcasts the mindset it's aiming to instill, and nomenclature can play a part in this. In the chapter "The Loop Mindset," we described other key aspects that must be included in the process itself: working with tensions, learning continually, and strengthening responsibility and trust.

THE BROADER TRANSFORMATION ARCHITECTURE

| | MONTH 1 | MONTH 2 | MONTH 3 | MONTH 4 | MONTH 5 | MONTH 6 | ... |

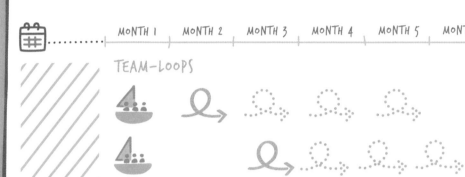

TEAM-LOOPS

SCOUTING & PREPARATION

STAKEHOLDER MANAGEMENT

TRANSFORMATION TEAM

LEADERSHIP LOOP

FACILITATOR TRAININGS

CONTENT & COMMUNICATION

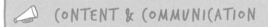

THE OPERATING SYSTEM

*I*n the previous chapter, we learned extensively about the anatomy and mechanics of a single Loop. But any broader transformation will require many more Loops beyond the first, as well as a few additional key components. That's why we'll now show you what the Loop Approach looks like when it's scaled up into a broader transformation architecture. As you'll soon discover, this requires a few workstreams to run alongside the Loops themselves.

SCOUTING AND PREPARATION

No transformation project worth its salt can be finished in just a few weeks or months. In the projects we undertake, we typically help our clients for an entire year, sometimes much longer. But before we can get started, we need to do a bit of scouting work to find the answers to the following questions:

- Why does the organization want to transform itself?
- What pain points is it trying to solve through the transformation?
- Has it defined a motivating future vision that the transformation is aimed at attaining?
- Are the employees on board and truly ready to change their own behavior?
- Is the leadership of the organization on board?
- Is it even realistic to undergo a successful transformation right now, or are there too many obstacles in the way?

We find it utterly fascinating that many organizations are steadfast in their desire to transform, but when asked, can't give a reason for why they want to. That's why, before starting the project, our first phase of work aims to develop a shared view of where the organization is right now, and where it roughly wants to be post-transformation. Only when all the above questions have been answered can we start planning the Loops and the transformation project in more detail.

We begin by putting together a project architecture like the one presented in the image above. It will take into account the unique current conditions of the organization, which influence what tools and methods we include in the Loops. This is where we challenge every element of the workshop, questioning whether it could be replaced with something even more useful. So, for example, if the organization isn't suffering from any transparency or synchronization issues in its teams, then we may choose to omit the sync meeting topic from the Loops.

Once the Loop has been defined, we then need to select the right teams to start the transformation. To aid us in picking these pioneers, we use the following guiding principles:

Volunteers only: No team should start a Loop just because someone else wants them to.

Apply within: It's good if the teams actually have to apply for the spots as the Loop pioneers, because this makes it seem like a scarce, and hence more desirable, opportunity. The transformation team should make the decision about who starts first.

BYOB (Bring-Your-Own-Budget): Consider carefully whether the participating teams should use their own budget for undergoing the Loop, or if if everyone can dip into a shared budget. The benefit of the former is that something is usually perceived as more valuable if you have to pay for it yourself.

Trail-blazing pioneers wanted: The teams undertaking the first Loops should be open-minded and eager to try something completely new.

Have a taste of your own medicine: As soon as possible, ideally even as the first pioneer team, the transformation team within the organization itself should also go through a Loop. This shows that they are leading by example and also gives them credibility in the eyes of others.

STAKEHOLDER MANAGEMENT

One crucial workstream in any transformation project is focused on manag-
ing key stakeholders. That's because there are always people who can help or
hinder the project, and you need to keep a close eye on them. We've seen many
transformation projects take unnecessary detours because powerful stakeholders were left out of the process, and as a result, put their considerable organizational muscle to work against the project. Stakeholder management is
a vital workstream to avoid this. Even though it's typically not very demand-
ing work-wise, it's crucial for success because it helps avoid nasty surprises.

To start this workstream, we use a simple method known as stakeholder mapping. All it requires is mapping all project stakeholders along two dimensions:

○ *How much power does this person or group of people have?*
○ *How favorable are they toward the transformation team and project?*

This method allows us to quickly identify the most important people and groups for the project—the key stakeholders. Next, we ask ourselves:

- *What existing communication channels can we use to reach each of these key stakeholders? For example, does someone in the transformation team already have a good relationship with them?*
- *What pragmatic and efficient ways can we think of to include these key stakeholders in the transformation process? For example, is it enough to just keep them updated via regular lunch meetings or is something more formal required?*

In the transformation team, it's often helpful to create one or several roles dedicated to dealing with each stakeholder. These roles can then provide brief updates regarding the stakeholders in the project teams' sync meetings, so that everyone knows what's going on.

THE LOOPS

With the preparations done and key stakeholders accounted for, we can get started with the actual Loops. The first team will take around 2—3 months to complete their Loop, supported and guided by two Loop trainers. First, we schedule workshops for the three modules and potentially also a preparatory module 0 (see more below). In between, the team itself takes responsibility for organizing and running recap sessions without the trainers.

Afterwards, the second team can start its Loop, typically with a small delay after the first team has finished theirs. This is so that the second team can benefit from the first team's experience. As mentioned before, the first team typically has the choppiest experience, but their learnings help still the waters for the teams that follow.

Typically, when supporting a client's transformation process, we guide the Loops for the first three to eight teams. Simultaneously, we also train internal people to support the process by first acting as co-trainers in our workshops before eventually becoming fully-fledged Loop trainers themselves. And as soon as they're ready to take over fully, we, the external trainers, are no longer needed in the workstream in question and try to leave the building gracefully before security escorts us out.

MODULE 0

Usually, a team can start Module 1 without any preparation. But still, many organizations prefer to set up preparatory sessions to ensure that each team is fully ready for the Loop. This is what Module 0 is for. Structured as a 2—3 hour workshop, it typically takes place in the week prior to Module 1 and has the following goals:

o The team learns what to expect from the Loop modules.
o The team takes stock of its current status using our scoreboard below, comprising the seven habits of highly effective organizations as dimensions. The team also sets developmental goals for each.

Module 0 is where we ensure that the team is really ready to start:

o Does everyone know what to expect? Are they ready for the shared journey?
o Is this really a team as per our definition, meaning a group of 4—12 people that spend most of their time at work pursuing a shared goal? Or is it more of an interest group or idea-sharing forum?

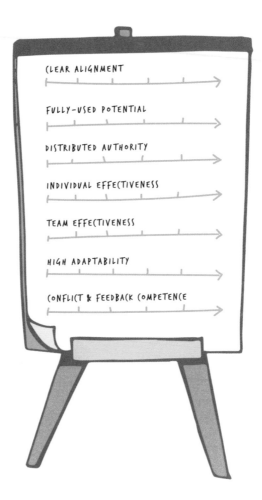

Taking stock of the status quo

At the beginning of Module 0, we analyze the status quo together with the team, as well as developing a shared view of where they could be by the end of the Loop. We do so by examining where the team currently stands in terms of each of the seven habits of highly effective organizations.

To get an objective picture, we ask each team member for their subjective view of the situation. They can indicate their opinion by placing small sticker dots on a board showing all seven habits as a left-to-right axes. Another option is for everyone to arrange themselves in a row according to where they currently see the team in terms of each habit.

What's our target here?

Next, the team needs to discuss the desired target level: "What would be the next sensible developmental step to improve our standing for this habit?" Of course, they may be tempted to try to leap straight to the ideal state for all seven dimensions at once, but this is no more attainable than it would be to get Arnold Schwarzenegger's 80s body by doing a single bicep curl. In fact, the positive extremes of the habits, like "We're 100% aligned around our shared purpose" should rather be seen as unachievable ideal goals. Hence, the question should instead be: "What's the next sensible evolutionary step we can take for each dimension that gets us one step closer to the ideal state?"

TRAININGS AND DEEP-DIVE MODULES

In addition to Module 0 and the actual Loop (Modules 1—3), we also offer additional trainings and modules around specific topics, like say NVC. There are endless options for these and it's up to the company to use its tensions to understand which ones it needs. Here, we'll present some of the most common ones.

Facilitator trainings

As mentioned before, we believe good meetings are one of the key aspects of effective organizations. And one crucial component of such meetings is enjoying great facilitation by people trained to provide it. That's why, in parallel to the Loops, we usually hold facilitator trainings. The cost is fairly low, since each team only needs 1—2 good facilitators, who can each facilitate meetings of up to ten people. In the Loop modules, it's usually clear who has a knack for this, and they can then deepen their skills by participating in the facilitator training. There, they will practice a broad range of skills ranging from employing useful facilitation phrases to demonstrating the right body language.

Deep-dive module on personal effectiveness

In the beginning of module 2, we focused on personal effectiveness to help the team find a shared GTD process and language for work. In many organizations though, we've found that differences in personal effectiveness between individuals can be huge: Some might be black-belt-level users of tools like GTD, already fully used to clearing their inboxes and thinking in terms of projects and next actions. Meanwhile, others might never even have asked themselves how to better organize their work. This is problematic, because for a team to work together in a truly effective way, all members need to be able to organize their work, as well as prioritize and synchronize with others. So we often suggest that teams also go through a deep-dive module on personal effectiveness, as it can really help the transformation process succeed. Typically, this module will be completely voluntary, with only those people choosing to participate who feel they really need to improve their ability to self-organize. In this deep-dive module, they will learn more about useful tools like *Getting Things Done* or *The 7 Habits of Highly Effective People*

Deep-dive module on nonviolent communication

NVC is an incredibly powerful tool. We've found that introducing this more effective and human-centered approach to communication can greatly boost any transformation effort, as well as help establish a culture of trust, support, connection, and humanness.

While NVC is ever-present in all our work, it plays a particularly big part in Module 2, where we deal with feedback and conflict. The learnings there provide a good starting point for teams, but typically, members will need a bit more time to really internalize the steps of the NVC process. That's why it often makes sense for them to attend a deep-dive module on the topic. What's more, many organizations we work with find NVC so valuable that they decide to go even further: they often send some of their employees to in-depth NVC trainings so that they can become fully-fledged trainers and mediators.

Deep-dive module on mindfulness

Cast your mind back to the Four Spaces model. There, the individual space doesn't seem to get as much explicit attention as in the Loop Approach. However, it does still play an important part: in the course of a Loop, we create many small mindfulness practices like check-ins and reflection rounds, where people are encouraged to be more mindful and listen to each other. As an organization undergoes these changes, it's not unusual for its members to realize that they want to dive deeper into the topics of mindfulness and empathy. As the success of programs like *Search Inside Yourself* demonstrate, these themes are currently front and center in the world of work. That's why we offer a deep-dive module on the topics of mindfulness and individual space, too.

THE LEADERSHIP LOOP

As stated before, no transformation can be successful unless the leadership is fully onboard and able to actively participate in the process. And future leaders will need completely new competencies to lead in the uncertain and constantly changing environments of tomorrow. In our own Loop organization, leaders are no longer there to manage employees and look over their shoulders to ensure they're doing their jobs right. Nor is their main goal to make all the decisions for others anymore. And we want to help the leaders at client companies to shed these responsibilities as well.

The Leadership Loop usually starts with assessing the status quo: What do the leaders do every day and what roles do they fulfill? (Hint: usually it's way too many.) What roles get the right amount of time and attention? (Hint: typically, the wrong ones.) What roles often take up a lot of time, even though they really shouldn't be a priority? And what roles could be easily delegated to the team to free up the leader's time for the truly important stuff?

As for the format, we've found that it's often useful to coach each leader individually, helping them map out the roles they currently fill. They can then decide which ones they should hang on to in the future, and which can be delegated to someone else. We also encourage the leaders to come up with completely new leadership roles that should get more attention in the future. To do so, they need to involve their team in the process, asking them: "What roles and tasks do leaders currently hold in our organization? Which of those should remain as the focus of leadership? Which shouldn't, and should rather be delegated to the teams?"

Three roles that are often touted as crucial in future leadership are:

Lead role

This role involves defining a compelling vision of the future, translating that vision into strategies, and getting everyone in the team on board and motivated to pursue them. It requires the leader to continuously evaluate what's happening both in- and outside of the organization and adapt the vision and strategy regularly.

Processes

This role is responsible for translating strategies and goals into good processes, asking every day: "What should we do next? What tactics and next steps are the right ones? Where do we need to adapt and remove obstacles?"

Coaching

This role ensures that all team members can grow, learn continuously, and harness their full potential.

Please note that the exact names of the roles vary in literature and between companies, these are just the labels we use.

Typically, in the Leadership Loop, we'll ask a few key leaders to develop a first prototype defining these leadership roles, which can then be used as standard ones to be introduced in each team. The prototype should embrace the Loop mindset, but also take into account the current status of the organization. It doesn't make sense to throw something useful overboard just because something new and shiny comes floating along!

Please note that the timing of the Leadership Loop is flexible: it can happen either before the teams start their Loops or in parallel to them.

CONTENT AND COMMUNICATION

Another important additional workstream needed to support the transformation project relates to content and communication. In our experience, providing useful additional content can provide a powerful boost to the transformation. All the new knowledge gained can be made accessible through online trainings, glossaries, wikis, or whatever other way works for the organization in question. This is also useful because not every team can be in a Loop simultaneously, but everyone can access knowledge if it's shared with them. That's why we always encourage clients to include this aspect in a workstream.

Another important aspect of a successful transformation is changing the language used in the organization to reflect the intended new mindset. That's why offering people useful new phrases via posters or other creative channels can be very effective. For example, one company we worked with used posters with questions like "What do you need?" or "Which one of my roles can you expect this from?" They even had a sticker in the bathroom suggesting: "Keep calm and mention your tension." Regardless of whether these attempts sound like they could be effective or appropriate in your organization, it definitely makes sense to include a workstream focused on communications in the transformation project. This way, it isn't just left up to chance whether the right messages and signals are sent to the organization at the right times. The workstream might decide, for example, that it would be useful for the leadership team to give regular updates on the status of the transformation. Or the transformation team could hold regular open office hours, where teams who haven't started a Loop yet could come in to get updated and learn from the experiences from previous Loops. And of course, there are countless other ways to ensure effective communication rearding the transformation. To find the right way for your transformation project, create a communications role in the transformation team and give it to someone who has a knack for transparency and communications. They'll figure it out, if you let them.

DIGITAL CONTENT HELPS
SCALING THE CHANGE PROJECT.

THE OPERATING SYSTEM

When transformations are discussed, the topic of a new Operating System (OS) usually gets a lot of attention. Some schools of thought, such as Holacracy, operate from an OS-first perspective, where the transformation follows from the OS. But we typically suggest the opposite approach: After the first Loops have been finished, around six months in, it can make sense to start codifying the new rules of the organization. By this time, it should be fairly clear which ones are actually being used and which ones don't make sense in real life. An OS should be minimalistic in the sense that it only contains what's actually used and lived in the organization, not what sounds nice or sensible but hasn't been picked up in vivo. If people just aren't embracing the new "Coffee is for closers!"-policy, it shouldn't go into the OS. Overall, we would advise you to keep your OS as slim as possible and ensure that everyone in the organization knows it by heart and adheres to it.

How you document your OS doesn't really matter. Most organizations already have tools for sharing knowledge that fit the bill, so definitely don't introduce some fancy new tool just for this purpose if everyone is already using something else. The goal is to make your OS easily accessible to everyone. What's more, as soon as the first version is ready, include it as part of the onboarding that new employees receive. And just as with other operating systems, it may well make sense to keep updating it regularly.

Any broader transformation process is complex, and its exact course is hard to predict in advance. It can be helpful to consider certain success factors, such as getting everyone in the organization on board with the transformation, especially the leadership.

The broader transformation architecture should include several workstreams, one being the actual Loops, where we work with the teams. This is supported by additional trainings, as well as stakeholder management and communications workstreams.

The leaders in the organization should be supported in the transformation through a specific Leadership Loop.

The transformation architecture should always be adapted to fit the specific needs of the organization in question.

A group of excellent people should form the transformation team within the organization. They must give the transformation their full focus and take responsibility for it.

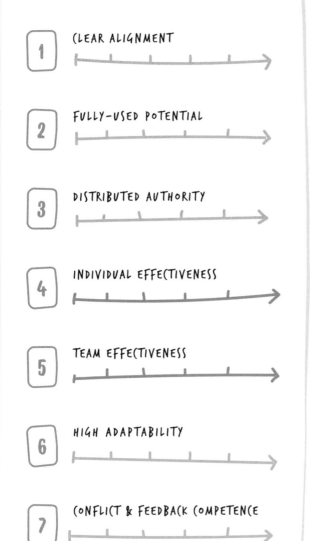

THE 7 HABITS OF HIGHLY EFFECTIVE ORGANIZATIONS

1 CLEAR ALIGNMENT

2 FULLY-USED POTENTIAL

3 DISTRIBUTED AUTHORITY

4 INDIVIDUAL EFFECTIVENESS

5 TEAM EFFECTIVENESS

6 HIGH ADAPTABILITY

7 CONFLICT & FEEDBACK COMPETENCE

THE

CLARITY

LOOP

RESULTS

EVOLUTION

SCOUTING &
PREPARATION

Individual Team Loops

Meetings

 STAKEHOLDER MANAGEMENT

TRANSFORMATION TEAM

LEADERSHIP LOOP

FACILITATOR TRAININGS

CONTENT AND COMMUNICATION

THE OPERATING SYSTEM

A s we said before, whenever we aim to do solid work, we start with a check-in. But importantly, we also end with a check-out. The check-out allows us to catch our breath, take a step back and reflect. Did we get what we needed out of this?

At the beginning of the book, we asked you what you would need from it in order to consider the time you invested into it a full success. At this point, we can only hope most of your expectations were met.

Ideally, it should by now be clear to you why the world of work is urgently in need of a transformation, but also why this is a great opportunity for all of us willing to participate in it. We don't know exactly what the organization of the future will look like, but the Loop Approach will help you begin your own transformation, and—together with your team—build your own version of it. It's just as important that you don't take this task too seriously: see it as a fun challenge, invite others to join you on your journey, and don't forget to enjoy yourself on the way! And if you find yourself unsure of how to get started or what the best next steps would be, we'd be more than happy to hear from you. Just drop us an email at hi@loopapproach.com

This last part of the book will provide you with some additional resources, like the books and online resources we consider the most relevant for you as well as our New Work Glossary. If this isn't enough to quench your thirst for knowledge on the topic, visit our website to see how we can get to know each other in a real-life (eek!) workshop: www.loopapproach.com.

And if you found this book helpful, please feel free to pass it on; perhaps someone else would benefit from reading it too!

But that's enough of our jabbering, it's time to get started. Good luck, we're in this together!

CHECKLIST FOR WORKSHOPS

FOR ALL LOOP WORKSHOPS, PLEASE ENSURE THE FOLLOWING:

- ☑ All team members are present, and their day is free for the workshop. If important calls have to be made, they should happen during the intervals.

- ☑ Ideally, there are two trainers for each Loop, at least one of whom is a seasoned Loop trainer.

- ☑ The workshop takes place at a location outside of the team's normal working environment. This ensures that the team members can fully immerse themselves in the new content without being distracted by their everyday work.

- ☑ The room for the workshop is a safe space—quiet and private enough that the team members don't need to worry about outside people listening in.

- ☑ The room allows the team to sit in one big circle where everyone can see each other. Also, people can walk around, stand, or sit together in small groups—a single big meeting table won't work here.

- ☑ The room has plenty of whiteboards, flipcharts, or walls that can be written on.

- ☑ Set up a tension stash, where everyone can save their tensions to be processed later. This can simply be a big "Tensions" post-it on the wall, below which everyone sticks smaller post-its with their actual tensions.

- ☑ Set up a next actions board, where next actions can be captured.

- ☑ Make the agenda for the day visible, for example on a flipchart, so that everyone knows what to expect.

- ☑ Have all standard workshop materials available, meanings things like a timer, post-its of all sizes, plenty of pens, glue sticks, scissors, Scotch Tape, a few thermoses full of Mimosa (not really) and so forth.

- ☑ Keep a sufficient supply of sugar-free drinks and insulin-friendly snacks, like nuts and fruit, for people to enjoy during the breaks.

- ☑ Lunch should be organized in a time-efficient way, and food should be light enough to avoid the dreaded post-prandial slump. People should be productive in the afternoon, not in a state of coma, napping on their colleagues' shoulders, and drooling on their post-its.

ADDITIONAL RESOURCES

You'll find loads of additional resources like handy cards for facilitating meetings
and workshop handouts on our website:

www.loopapproach.com

Reading list

Below, you'll find the most important books that helped us develop the Loop Approach:

Allen, D. (2015). *Getting Things Done: The Art of Stress-free Productivity*. Revised. New York: Penguin.

Anderson, D.; Ackerman Anderson, L. (2010). *Beyond Change Management. How to achieve Breakthrough Results through Conscious Change Leadership*. 2nd Edition. San Francisco: Pfeiffer.

Beck, D.E.; Cowan, C.C. (2005) *Spiral Dynamics—Mastering Values, Leadership and Change*. Malden: Wiley-Blackwell.

Brown, T. (2009). *Change by Design. How Design Thinking can transform Organizations and inspires Innovation*. New York: Harper Collins.

Collins, J. (2001). *Good to great. Why Some Companies make the Leap... and others Don't*. New York: Harper Collins.

Covey, S. R. (2013). *The 7 Habits of Highly Effective People. Powerful Lessons in Personal Change.* 25th Edition. New York: Simon & Schuster.

Dignan, A. (2019). *Brave New Work. Are you ready to reinvent your organization?* New York: Portfolio/Penguin.

Ismail, S.; Malone, M. S.; van Geest, Y. (2014). *Exponential Organizations. Why New Organizations are Ten Times better, faster, and cheaper than yours (and what to do about it).* New York: Diversion Books.

Laloux, F. (2014). *Reinventing Organizations. A Guide to Creating Organizations inspired by the Next Stage of Human Consciousness.* Brussels: Nelson Parker.

Robertson, B. J. (2015). *Holacracy. The New Management System for a Rapidly Changing World.* New York: Henry Holt and Company.

Rosenberg, M. B. (2015). *Nonviolent Communication. A Language of Life.* 3rd Edition. Encinitas: PuddleDancer Press.

Scharmer, O. (2016). *The Theory U. Leading from the Future as it Emerges. The Social Technology of Presencing.* 2nd Edition. Oakland: Berrett-Koehler Publishers.

Sinek, S. (2009). *Start with Why: How great Leaders Inspire Everyone to Take Action.* New York: Penguin.

Sutherland, J. (2014). *Scrum. The Art of Doing Twice the Work in Half the Time.* New York: Crown Business.

Tan, C.-M. (2012). *Search Inside Yourself. The Unexpected Path to Achieving Success, Happiness (and World Peace).* New York: Harper One.

New Work Glossary

Accountability

If you're accountable for something, it means that others can count on you to take care of it. And when an organization wants to make responsibilities crystal clear, it often makes sense to define recurring tasks as accountabilities and then package them into roles. Recurring tasks could include things like: "Makes all salary payments to employees" or "Ensures all the lights in the office are turned off for the night." In this way, accountabilities constitute the smallest building blocks of an organization, reflecting all the recurring tasks that need to be performed in it.

Advice Process

This is a decision-making process first introduced by Frédéric Laloux in his book → *Reinventing Organizations*. Similar to the → *Integrative Decision Making* process from → *Holacracy*, the Advice Process enables you to integrate all relevant perspectives into a decision without having to build → *consent*. The way it works is that one person creates a proposal, asks for relevant → *feedback* and then integrates all potential → *objections* into the proposal. Typically, feedback should be requested from everyone who either has relevant information for the decision or who will be significantly affected by it. After this, the person who initiated the process makes a decision, informing everyone else of the outcome.

Agility

A term originally coined in the world of software development, *agile* denotes a new kind of collaboration model that is meant to replace the old waterfall model, where a fixed plan is made and rigorously followed. In agile work, the basis for work is rather a shared understanding of the desired outcome of a project, whereas the plan to get there gets continuously recalibrated. And in case you're wondering about the difference between agility and flexibility: Something is flexible if it can reactively change its shape and bounce back to its original form later. Meanwhile, something is agile if it can proactively change its shape when the external requirements change, and go on to maintain this new form in the future.

Ambidexterity, organizational

Literally, ambidexterity means being not just right- or left-handed, but rather two-handed. In organizational literature, this is also sometimes referred to as the buzzword-y concept *exploit vs. explore*. An ambidextrous organization is one that's able to provide space, simultaneously, for two completely different types of work: innovation and the efficient implementation of existing processes. The former, called exploration, requires a risk-seeking mindset and boldly trying out new ideas while suppressing critical thinking. Meanwhile, the latter, unflatteringly called exploitation, focuses on failure prevention, efficiency and processes in familiar territory, requiring a mindset that encourages seeking and voicing mistakes and inefficiencies. Clearly, each requires a very different way of thinking, which is why true ambidexterity is not easy for most organizations to attain.

Authority

The right to exercise power by making significant decisions in an organization.

Autocracy

From the ancient Greek for "self power." autocracy typically describes a situation where one person rules over others, holding all the power to make decisions. In the context of the Loop Approach, using → *roles* is sometimes referred to as distributed autocracy. This is due to the fact that roles can make autocratic decisions within their own domains. In other words, while a role can always ask for feedback and input from others, it can also make a decision without them agreeing with it.

Check-in and Check-out

These are two simple yet effective rituals for → *meetings*. The check-in provides everyone the space to arrive, unload emotional baggage and become fully present. Typical questions for the check-in session are: "What's on my mind?" and "What has my attention right now?" In a check-out session, the goal is to conclude the meeting and reflect on it in order to learn for the future. Typical questions for the check-out session include: "What's on my mind as I leave the meeting?" or "What would I like to see done differently in the next meeting?"

Circle Model

In contrast to the → *pyramid* and → *matrix organization*, the circle model doesn't depict the organization as boxes, but rather as circles containing smaller circles and dots for roles within them. Using roles instead of individuals as the smallest unit displayed in this visualization has the benefit that you can also see how single individuals can fulfill multiple roles across several circles. One well-known example of this model being used is → *Holacracy*.

Clear the Air (CTA)

A meeting type based on → *Nonviolent Communication*, CTA meetings focus on voicing and resolving all the interpersonal tensions present in a → *team* by using a mirroring technique. Rather than resulting in concrete outcomes, the goal of the CTA meeting is to foster mutual understanding, thereby strengthening the relationships of participants and hence the team as well.

Communication

See → *language*

Conflict

Working with → *people* usually means also dealing with conflict from time to time. By conflict, we don't mean a situation where people merely have differing views on a topic, but rather that their perspectives also seem totally incompatible with each other—at least at first sight. Usually conflicts also involve a strong emotional component, and they put a strain on interpersonal relationships. Models like → *NVC* can help resolve conflicts in a constructive way. In NVC, this is done by clearly distinguishing between the level of facts and the interpersonal relationship.

Coach

The coach → *role* is one that's getting more and more attention in organizations lately. A coach's main job is to create space for coachees where they can reflect on themselves and their own development. The coach facilitates their growth by asking questions, enabling them to, for example, become more → *mindful* or improve their → *leadership* skills. Some organizations opt to create a standard coach role in every circle or → *team*. This is meant to ensure that this important aspect of work gets enough attention throughout the organization.

Command and Control

See → *mindset*

Consensus

A → *decision-making* principle where decisions can only be made if everyone member of the group agrees with it. This is not to be mixed up with → *consent.*

Consent

A → *decision-making* principle that doesn't require people to agree to the decision, in contrast to the → *consensus* or → *majority* principles. Rather, consent only focuses on disagreement, meaning → *objections*. If objections are raised, they must be integrated into the proposal by the person objecting and the person who made the original proposal. In other words, these two are responsible for finding a new solution that takes the objection into consideration.

Culture

In the context of work, culture usually means the shared values, norms and beliefs that are present in an organization and which influence collective behavior. The importance of culture is perhaps best summed up by Peter Drucker's quote: *"Culture eats strategy for breakfast."* In other words, building a strong culture can wield a much greater impact on an organization's success than forging even the smartest strategy. But what's often forgotten is that changing an organization's culture is a tremendous challenge. And contrary to what many leaders seem to believe, merely writing down the intended values and publishing them as a manifesto to rarely has the desired impact.

Definition of Done (DoD)

A tool from the → *agile* toolbox that's meant to improve collaboration by defining clearly and measurably when a project has been finished. This is especially important for agile teams, because their plans are in constant flux. In order for the path to be easily malleable, the shared end goal must be crystal-clear for everyone, with no room for interpretation as to when it has been achieved.

Decision-making

Having → *authority* usually entails the ability and obligation to make decisions. Therefore, if the goal is to distribute authority through the organization in a less hierarchical way, new decision-making principles are needed. Even simple changes can help, like introducing the → *consent* principle or the idea of declaring → *intent* instead of asking for approval.

Design Thinking

Simultaneously a collection of tools as well as a → *mindset*, the original ideal behind Design Thinking was to take the way that product designers work and apply it to all kinds of problems. Key elements of Design Thinking include shoving egos aside and putting the user front and center: what's really the best solution for a problem from a user perspective? This requires a better understanding of people and their needs in general. Other important aspects of Design Thinking include embracing different perspectives and bringing up as many ideas as possible, all the while continuously building, changing, testing and discarding assumptions.

Digitalization

Sometimes also called the fourth industrial revolution, what we mean by digitalization in the world of → *organizations* are the changes that are happening due to new digital tools. On the one hand, this means the actual digitalization of processes, like an office going paperless and using new digital tools to, for example, edit audio content. On the other hand, it also means a completely new way of working, because new digital tools have led to faster-changing, more complex business environments. They require organizational models that are more → *agile*, adaptive and → *self-organized*.

Domain

The area of responsibility that a → *role* controls, including both concrete and abstract things, like budgets or decisions around a certain topic.

Double Linking

A principle originally introduced in → *Sociocracy*, double linking means that all circles or teams should always have two connections to the outside world: one on the inside and one on the outside. The inside → *role*, referred to as the → *lead* role in → *Holacracy*, is in charge of receiving information from the outside and processing it within the circle, for example by setting new strategies or proposing

new roles to be created. Meanwhile, the outside role captures all the → *tensions* that arise in the circle but which can't be resolved there, and escalates them to the greater circle outside. There, the tensions may be resolved by, for example, allocating additional resources to dealing with them or asking another circle to help out.

Ego

In a scientific sense, the ego is what we call the "I" or the "self." But when we talk about egos in the context of work, we usually mean people putting themselves before the goals or → *purpose* of a team or organization. Many organizations are now beginning to realize that to attain their goals, they need less ego and more → *mindfulness* and → *emotional competencies*.

Election

Just as in politics, elections can be used in organizations to match → *people* with → *roles*. Typically, whenever there's an election in a circle, each circle member gets one vote. There are a few differences to political elections though. For example, in → *Holacracy*, the votes are not secret, and in fact, each vote has to be publicly justified. What's more, after the first round of voting and justifications, everyone can still change their vote. Typically, the result of the election can only be effectively enacted if the person elected actually accepts the outcome.

Emotional Competence

The capacity to recognize feelings in yourself and others, as well as being able to influence them. Emotional competence has to do with → *mindfulness* and empathy, meaning the ability to put yourself in the position of others. This is relevant in the world of work, because compassion, meaning the desire to alleviate suffering in others, and, more precisely, compassionate leadership, is often hailed as a key capability in the future of leadership.

Empowerment

A way to distribute → *responsibility* more evenly across an organization, empowerment as a term is sometimes criticized for its hierarchical connotations. It implies that someone holds power and empowers others by deciding to share some of it. A → *role-based* organization works differently: all power is divided up into roles, which are then distributed among the members of the organization. That's why, in a role-based organization, empowerment is basically a given and no longer has to be done by superiors.

Facilitator

A key → *role* that helps make → *meetings* more effective, a facilitator focuses the participants' attention on whatever best serves the meeting's purpose. In a clearly-defined meeting format, like the → *sync meeting* or the → *governance* meeting, the facilitator follows the goals of the meeting and an agreed-upon structure. To this end, the facilitator can ask questions, allow participants to speak and cut them off when necessary. In general, the facilitator uses communication and body language to guide the meeting to its intended outcome.

Feedback

In the context of work, feedback constitutes all the responses that someone receives that can help them reflect on and change their behavior. Feedback can be given not only between peers, but also bi-directionally from different levels of a hierarchy. It can focus on performance, for example in → *roles*, or it can

aim at something else, like personal development. The more → *responsibility* is distributed within an organization, the more important feedback becomes, because otherwise people won't have a realistic view of how their work and behavior is perceived by others. To ensure adequate feedback, often all teams in an organization set up specific feedback → *meetings*.

Four Spaces

This model was first introduced by Tom Thomison, one of the co-founders of HolacracyOne. He differentiates the four spaces of human interaction as follows: The operational space is where all the actual work happens, meaning things like exchanging information and the completion of tasks. The governance space is where the structure of the organization can be changed by, for example, creating new rules and roles. In addition, there are also two spaces that focus on human relationships: The individual space is where self-reflection, personal growth and emotional processes occur, and the tribe space is where interpersonal relationships and the corresponding conflicts reside. The main point of the four spaces model is that it enables you to figure out which of the spaces is best suited to solve a given tension, so that you can pick the right method for doing so.

Getting Things Done (GTD)

A productivity system introduced by David Allen, GTD takes many common-sense ideas about productivity, such as thinking in terms of projects and → *next actions*, and combines them into a comprehensive system. The goal is to ensure "stress-free productivity," or a "mind like water." To clarify the latter, it means having a mind that responds to external stimuli like water responds to a stone falling into it: always with exactly the appropriate reaction, no bigger or smaller than required, with the surface rapidly becoming calm again afterward.

Goals

In general, goals can be described as assumptions about what should be achieved in the future. Setting goals can help focus people's behavior in a way that helps in attaining the intended outcome. Especially in large organizations, goals can help avoid wasting energy on misalignments. The clearer a goal is, the easier it usually is to work toward it. To ensure unified efforts on the organizational level, different parts of an organization need to synchronize their goals and align them around the greater goals of the overall organization. And this is only possible if every level of the organization, including the organization itself, has clearly defined goals. Finally, goals are not set in stone: especially in → *agile* organizations operating in complex and ever-changing environments, goals have to be frequently adjusted to reflect new realities.

Governance meeting

Introduced in → *Holacracy,* the governance meeting format is used to make decisions that affect the structure of the organization, not the operational work. This can mean creating new → *roles* or rules, or changing existing ones. To make these structural decisions, the → *IDM* is used. In general, you could say that in the governance meeting, people don't work *in* the organization, but rather *on* the organization.

Heuristic

A rule of thumb that enables decisions to be made with limited information and often time too. Heuristics tend to reduce complexity by simplifying

complicated matters into straightforward rules, like "if A, then always do B." The danger of these simplifications is that they can lead to mistakes, but in complex environments, they often still make sense by allowing decisions to be made when it's impossible to define a comprehensively logical solution. The human brain also relies on heuristics to save computational power and make decisions more efficiently. In the context of → *strategy,* heuristics can be used to make → *prioritization* decisions in a decentralized system. For example, "*A>B,*" *"speed over perfection"* and *"customer satisfaction over revenue"* are all examples of heuristics that would allow for rapid strategic decisions even under great uncertainty. Of course, if an organization's strategy and priorities change, so do the heuristics used to translate that strategy into behavior.

Hierarchy

An ordering principle of an organization, where people are placed in levels with those on higher ones controlling those below. People sometimes falsely assume that new organizational models like → *Holacracy* have completely done away with hierarchy, but this is actually not true. What typically happens is that a hierarchy of → *people* is replaced by a hierarchy of → *roles.* And this increases complexity, because the new role hierarchy will be context dependent: If something happens in a → *domain* of role A, then this particular role has the authority to decide what to do about it. But if something happens in the domain of role B, then role B is at the top of the decision-making hierarchy in that situation.

Holacracy

An → *operating system* for organizations that's based on, among other things, → *Sociocracy* and → *Getting*

Things Done. Originally developed in the world of software development, Holacracy gets a lot of attention in the → *New Work* movement today. Nevertheless, only very few larger organizations have fully adopted it so far.

Human Resources (HR)

in the business world, HR is often used as a term to denote the human assets of an organization, meaning the people, their qualifications and the knowledge they possess. This perspective often stands at odds with a more human-centered view of organizations, which is based on the idea that people *are* the organization, rather than just a resource for it to use. This discrepancy is one reason why many organizations avoid the old term HR and instead create a people circle to deal with the relevant topics.

Integration

In the context of → *decision-making*, integration means combining two different perspectives into something new. For example, in the → *integrative decision-making process* in → Holacracy, an → *objection* against a proposal has to be integrated into it. This happens by having the person who objected and the person who made the original proposal find a new proposal together that resolves both the objection and the original → *tension.*

Integrative Decision Making (IDM)

An important tool for making decisions in a group, IDM uses the → *consent* principle, which is based on → *objections.* IDM allows a group to quickly come up with and further develop proposals by integrating different perspectives and potential objections along the way, with the end goal of getting to a usable outcome.

Intent

In traditional organizations, employees can rarely make meaningful decisions without first getting approval from their superiors. The notion of declaring intent turns this dynamic on its head: rather than asking for approval, the employee just has to declare their intent to make a decision (think: "I will do X...") and ask for → *objections.* This way, the employee gets more → *responsibility.* The idea was popularized in the book *Turn the Ship Around*, where it was introduced as a simple way to increase → *empowerment* in an organization.

Job title

In contrast to → *roles,* job titles are usually fixed and relatively inflexible. Everyone has one job title that describes what tasks they do as well as their level in the hierarchy. Some companies really seem to love job titles, going beyond the traditional Senior Vice Presidents, and introducing novel ones like Senator, Emperor, or Donut. (We admit we're more than a little jealous about the business card possibilities for that last one.)

Language

Now that grunting and pointing are mostly no longer considered socially acceptable communication (barring Mondays), language is the most important tool that → *people* use in the context of work. Some authors even go as far as to say that work today basically *is* language: We communicate via email, presentations, and digital tools like Slack, and sit in → *meetings* where we talk and listen. If we need to talk to machines, we use the language of code. And no matter whether it makes up 50, 80, or 100 percent of our work, the language we use still clearly warrants attention, and using language more → *mindfully* makes sense.

Lead role

Formerly called a lead link, this is one of the standard → *roles* in → *Holacracy*. It replaces the old manager role and is responsible for keeping the circle's → *purpose* in mind, as well as developing → *strategies* and setting → *priorities* for the circle. The lead role also gives performance → *feedback* to circle members, assigns roles to → *people,* and makes decisions affecting the resources and → *domains* that the circle controls, unless they are directly assigned to one of the roles in the circle. A central difference between the lead role and a traditional manager role is that the lead role cannot interfere with the autonomy granted to the roles in the circle. In other words, the lead role can define the priorities and give feedback, but it can't tell any of the circle members what to do and when to do it. Other differences are that some of the aspects of a traditional manager role have been split off into other roles, like the → *Facilitator* and → *Secretary* roles.

Leadership

Describes all the activities that are intended to lead or guide others in the → *organization*, providing direction. Traditionally, leadership was always packaged into → *manager* roles, but today, many organizations opt for → *distributed leadership* instead, where leadership occurs everywhere in the organization, based on roles.

Manager

This is a big word with many possible meanings and a lot of speculation as to what exactly it entails. An oft-held view stemming from a desire for efficient division of labour is that managers take responsibility for planning and supervising processes, whereas employees are responsible for the actual implementation. Nowadays, even the smallest units in an organizations, from tea kitchens to bathrooms, can have their own managers, which is why more creative → *job titles*, like Senior Yoga Mat Procurement Manager, are now en vogue. In general, the manager title hit its zenith in the 1980s and has since then lost some its allure and sway.

Management studies

A field of academia that focuses on the way businesses are operated, and how organizations in the business world tick. Some authors believe that the field focuses too heavily on → *money* and financial outcomes and too little on → *people*, resulting in the students of this topic getting a skewed view.

Matrix organization

Unfortunately, this has nothing to do with Keanu Reeves. Rather, the matrix model is the answer that classical → *management studies* offered to the question of how existing methods could be used to tackle increasingly complex external challenges. A matrix organization typically has two axes, going from top to bottom and from left to right, or vice versa. This means each employee can have two bosses, on both the vertical and the horizontal axes. This is in contrast to the → *pyramid*, which is only organized from top to bottom. Some claim that the visualization used for matrix organizations can also be used to depict even more complex network structures, such as the → *circle model*. This would require introducing additional dimensions, first turning the matrix into a cube and then into an n-dimensional geometric figure.

Meetings

Generally put, a meeting is any get-together of two or more people in the context of work. More specifically, it's a (potentially recurring) event where people from one or several teams meet in order to exchange information, make decisions and develop ideas and concepts. Often, no concrete work results are produced in the course of a meeting, which is why many feel that no actual → *work* gets done during meetings. And yet, in most organizations, practically everyone spends the majority of their time in meetings. On the one hand, this can lead to → *tensions* such as: "We spend too much time in meetings." But on the other hand, it means that therein also lies a great opportunity: making small improvements to meetings, such as introducing a → *facilitator* role, can greatly improve both the productivity and → *motivation* of a team or organization.

Mindfulness

Mindfulness is getting more and more attention in the professional world, and in → *New Work* circles in particular. It means the ability to more consciously perceive oneself and the world around, and it helps people change they way they work and act. Being mindful means being fully present, focusing on oneself and others, and just perceiving them without judging. Practices such as mindfulness meditation can help people explore themselves and become more connected to and conscious of the own thoughts and emotions.

Mindset

A central belief system which → *people* use to view themselves and the world around them. A mindset can also be embedded in an organizational → *operating system*. In this book, we make the point that the old mindset that most organizations still adhere to is called *predict and control* or *command and control*. But now, it is being replaced by a new mindset called *sense and respond*. Under the old mindset, → *managers*

made plans and controlled their implementation using a clear command hierarchy. But the new mindset relies on a different kind of planning: a clear, shared vision is defined, but the concrete goal and the path to get there are continually adjusted in response to new information coming in from the changing external environment. This new mindset typically works best in less hierarchical, more decentralized organizations.

Motivation

Motivation is usually further differentiated into intrinsic and extrinsic motivation. Intrinsic motivation means that something, for example work, is motivating in and of itself. Meanwhile, extrinsic motivation means that some external incentive, for example money, is the source of motivation to perform the work. The relative importance of these two depends on the → *mindset* prevalent in the organization. On one extreme, some might believe that people can only be truly productive if offered external motivation. On the other extreme, some feel that everyone already has enough internal drive and enthusiasm to motivate themselves at work. And some scholars argue that our educational system tends to train people to ignore intrinsic motivation and focus mainly on extrinsic motivation. The upshot is that it takes a fair bit of unlearning and learning before these people can work in a in a self-organized system without a → *manager* offering them extrinsic motivation in the form of carrots and sticks.

Next Actions

In David Allen's productivity system → *Getting Things Done*, a next action is the smallest possible unit of work. A next action means a task that's so small that it can be done in one sitting without much effort, typically in less than an hour. What's more, it's so concrete that it needs no further explanation or clarification. This means the name of the task must be descriptive and non-ambiguous: "Respond to the client's email by sending pre-prepared initial offer" or "Find a time-slot for peer feedback with Adam." According to David Allen, taking the time to write down exactly what the next action is in concrete terms, rather than just labeling vaguely with something like "Adam" is crucial. It may take more time initially but actually saves time later and makes work much more productive.

New Work

Originally coined by Frithjof Bergmann in the 1970s, the term "New Work" is today often used differently than he intended. Bergmann envisioned a completely new understanding of work, where people would overcome the slavery of wage labor and enjoy more spare time to participate in their communities and society. In a similar vein, authors like Frederic Laloux and schools of thought such as → *Spiral Dynamics* question our entire current understanding of work. They argue that humanity is in the process of moving toward a higher level of consciousness, which involves a different view of work as well. Looking at the term in a broader sense, New Work is often used today to denote anything related to → *digitalization* and its impact on the way people work in organizations. This is ironic, because some authors argue that digitalization is actually driving us to a way of working that, in the worst case, would constitute pretty much the opposite of Bergmann's vision. This would be the case if work continues to increasingly swallow up people whole, leaving less and less time and space for communities and participation. In that sense, the only difference digitalization has made is that work today is increasingly being performed remotely, from home.

Nonviolent communication (NVC)

A model for more effective and human-centered communication based on the work of Marshall B. Rosenberg, NVC focuses on human needs and their fulfillment, as well as on empathetic communication and appreciation of others. Many organizations have found NVC a useful tool in transforming the → *language* they use, which plays a key part in the overall transformation toward a more decentralized, human-centered organization.

Objectives and Key Results (OKR)

A system for → *goal* setting that has recently found increasing popularity even though it actually dates back to 1983, when Andy Grove first published a book on how Intel was using OKRs. The reason why it has again become so popular is probably that starting in 1999, Google discovered and started experimenting with the system. The key idea of OKRs is that an organization sets a small number of objectives for a relatively short interval of time, say, a single quarter. These objectives reflect the broader goals that the organization will focus on, and they should be fairly abstract, in the vein of: "Increase reach in social media." These can then be broken down into around three key results each, which must be measurable but so ambitious as to be unattainable. This means that reaching just 60% of a KR target could already constitute a stellar performance. The reason for setting unreachable goals is that every now and then something incredible happens and the impossible turns out to have been possible. OKRs are not meant to be used for performance reviews, even though some companies erroneously do so.

Objection

In the context of organizations, this concept was originally introduced as a part of → *Sociocracy*. There, objecting means that a member of a group can veto a proposal if they feel it will cause harm to the group. This then leads to the proposal not passing in its original form. Instead, it has to be changed (→ *integration*), so that the objection is no longer valid. It's worth noting that mere criticism or voicing a potentially better idea does not yet constitute a valid objection. In → *Holacracy*, the validity of objections is tested with the question: "Is it safe enough to try?" If the answer is yes, the objection is not valid.

Operating System (OS)

Inspired by how software operating systems work, sometimes the term OS is used in the context of organizations to describe the "rules of the game," meaning the way the organization is working. A well-known example of an operating system is → *Holacracy*, which uses a constitution to distribute → *authority* throughout the organization, defining how decisions are made, how meetings are structured, and so forth. Holacracy has rules for everything, including for when processes break down: "If process A doesn't work, use process B." Sometimes, people may also use OS to refer to the more abstract ideas by which an organization is governed. Hence, the term can mean anything from a strict codification of all the rules of the organization to a more general description of its values.

Organization

In the context of work, this term typically has two meanings: First, it's a group of two or more people pursuing a shared goal or interest, which means that they have to find a way to organize themselves to do so efficiently. In this sense, an organization can be anything from two friends joining forces to organize a party up to a multinational corporation with hundreds of thousands of employees. And the latter could also be broken down into countless sub-organizations. Second, the term "organization" also denotes the way people organize themselves, for example by using a hierarchical organization or → *self-organization*. To clarify the difference, let's try using both of these meanings in a single sentence: "Organizing an organization is a challenge that increases in difficulty with the size of the organization."

People

In → *business studies*, people are sometimes coldly referred to as "human capital." But many authors feel that people are in fact not just a resource used by the organization, but rather are the organization. People can be seen as paradoxical beasts: Thanks to our large brains, we are generally capable of rational thought and making decisions based on facts and data. But at the same time we're driven by emotions and operate in a fundamentally different way than machines. Many organizations assume that people can best be → *motivated* with → *money* or that they need to be reigned in and controlled to keep them from doing things that would harm the organization. But in the context of → *New Work*, it is becoming increasingly clear that people can also be motivated intrinsically if they find → *purpose* in their work and have interests that overlap with those of the organization. Of course, for people to find that purpose, the organization also needs to have one—beyond just generating profits.

Power

A term that often carries negative connotations, like that power can be too concentrated in a small group of individuals, it can be abused or it can corrupt → *people* into becoming increasingly → *ego*-driven. A more neutral view of the term would be to see power as a facet of → *responsibility*, where power means making → *decisions* and getting things done. → *New Work* authors often claim that responsibility and power should be more evenly distributed among the people in an organization.

Predict and Control

See → *Mindset*

Proactive Behavior

In contrast to reactive behavior, proactive behavior anticipates what will happen in the future and is focused on attaining certain targets. Mere activity is not necessarily target-focused, but proactivity always is. The term was popularized by Stephen Covey's book *The 7 Habits of Highly Effective People*, but it was used well before then, for example by Viktor Frankl in the 1940s. Based on his own experience surviving a Nazi concentration camp, Frankl described how to consciously steer one's own behavior and thoughts to break free from the purely reactive stimulus-response chain that most people live by.

Priorities

From the Latin "prior," meaning "former," priority means something that must get your attention, even if this means overriding other things. Originally, it didn't even have a plural form. In other words, there could only be one priority, one thing that precedes everything else. In the context of work, priorities often mean a small number of action areas, or → *goals* set in such areas. The idea there is that all or most of the attention available should be focused on those priorities. The fact that it was originally intended as

a singular but today is mostly used in the plural is indicative of the main challenge in setting and sticking to priorities: it's difficult to limit focus to one or a few things, especially in these times of complexity and rapidly changing environments. One way to overcome this challenge is to keep priorities flexible and change them continuously, for example through a system like → *OKRs*.

Prototype

In the context of → *teamwork*, a prototype means a first draft of something that will be iterated on further. More generally, it means a non-perfected version of something that can be developed further. One important aspect of working with prototypes is making the first versions visible and tangible as early as possible, so that people can give → *feedback* on them. Some authors even go so far as to claim that if one wants to have a work culture that emphasizes the continuous development and ego-free discussion of ideas, everything should always be considered a prototype.

Purpose

Meant here in the deeper sense, beyond just goals or strategy, the term often also includes a spiritual component. The concept helps organizations reflect on the question of why they exist in the world and why they are needed. Often a purpose is also considered an ideal goal that can never be truly achieved. In contrast to typical short-term goals, where the timeline may be just a few months, striving for the purpose is an infinite, never-ending endeavour. And uncovering the purpose is not just an exercise for organizations—teams and individuals can do it too by asking questions like "Why are we needed in this organization?," What is our contribution?," and

"Why am I needed in the world?" For an organization, the purpose is both the great common denominator uniting people and the engine driving the organization forward. It answers questions like "Why do we exist? What difference do we want to make in the world?" If an organization has a clear purpose, it's easy for people to check if said purpose is in line with what they want spend their time and energy on supporting.

Pyramid

This is the image most often used to visualize hierarchical organizational models in a relatively simple way. In a pyramid, people are placed in a clear hierarchy of levels, making it clear who stands where, who can make which decisions and who is authorized to order whom around. A slightly more complex version of this is the → *matrix organization* model. Underlying both of these is a notion of every person having a well-defined spot in a hierarchy, so it's totally clear who someone's boss and their boss's boss is.

Reinventing Organizations

The title of a 2014 book by Belgian author Frederic Laloux, it is often considered a milestone in the → *New Work* movement. The book presents several case studies researched by the author, describing organizations that work completely differently compared to traditional, hierarchical ones. Drawing on these, Laloux presents his theory that these different organizations are distinguished by three main characteristics: First, they → *self-organize*. Second, they enable wholeness, meaning that → *people* can show up to work as their full selves, without putting on any kind of front. Third, they are organized around an evolutionary → *purpose*.

Responsibility

A big word in the context of work, and often used in ambiguous ways. What exactly does it mean to be responsible for something, like a project or business area? How exactly are areas of responsibility demarcated? Defining clear answers to these questions makes it easier for people to collaborate effectively. One way to define responsibility is to bundle it into → *roles* by clustering → *accountabilities*. These roles can then be assigned to people, making it clear who is responsible for what. In hierarchical organizations, responsibility often goes hand in hand with → *power*, which tends to be concentrated at the top of the → *pyramid* and delegated from there.

Resources

The means that an organization can use to achieve its → *goals*. For companies, this is often understood as primarily their financial resources, but it also includes the knowledge and skills in the organization. In → *business studies*, people tend to be counted among these resources, which is why we have the concept of → *Human Resources*. The goal of a → *strategy* is to harness the resources of the organization in a way that enables the most effective pursuit of its goals.

Roles

A concept in many organizations that allows for → *responsibility* to be distributed in an organization by assigning roles to people. In → *Holacracy*, roles are clusters of accountabilities, united by a shared purpose of those accountabilities. These roles are flexible, changing all the time through a → *governance* process. In its most minimalistic incarnation, a role just has a name, a purpose, and at least one accountability, meaning one recurring task it performs. This could be something as simple as "Signs letters of reference" or "Sweeps yard."

Salary

A hot-button topic in any organization, salary is also much discussed in the → *New Work* movement. When → *responsibility* is more evenly distributed throughout an organization, there often also arises a desire to make salaries transparent and → *self-organized*. This can sometimes lead to → *tensions* and problems, especially if the organization tries to approach this difficult topic before learning how to effectively solve tensions and → *conflict*.

Scrum

An → *agile* methodology that originally emerged in the world of software development, scrum is nowadays often used in other contexts as well. Basically, it aims to make complex projects manageable by using a small set of rules and three standard → *roles*. It's based on the assumption that once a project reaches a certain level of complexity, extensive planning no longer makes sense. In these cases, rather than planning too carefully, it's much more effective to use short-term targets and delegate as many decisions as possible to the → *self-organizing* scrum team.

Search Inside Yourself

Originally developed by Chade-Meng Tan at Google, the Search Inside Yourself program is aims at helping people become more mindful, effective and happier. It does so by teaching them to be more present in the here and now. This eventually makes them better leaders, more successful in their careers and happier in general. The program was designed specifically for the business world, and the exercises involved are fast, easy and immediately rewarding, making them very easy to adopt.

Secretary

A role used in, for example, → *Holacracy*, the secretary takes on a part of what is traditionally folded into the leader's responsibilities: the documentation, tracking and interpretation of work results, decisions made in meetings, and the governance structure of an organization. Though sometimes underrated, this role has quite a bit of → *power*, and having the right person fill it can make a team considerably more effective.

Self-organization

In the context of → *New Work*, self-organization is often used to describe all kinds of collaboration that don't rely on top-down planning and hierarchical control. In other words, self-organized systems organize themselves from the inside out. In them, responsibilities and rules for decision-making are often transparent and based on individual competencies. For self-organization to work, it typically requires strong alignment around a shared greater goal, such as a → *purpose*.

Self-responsibility

In the context of → *work*, self-responsibility means taking → *responsibility* for oneself and one's own feelings and responses. This means, for example, bringing up and resolving → *tensions*. It also means adopting a → *proactive* rather than reactive mindset.

Sense and Respond

See → *mindset*

Sociocracy

An organizational model originally developed in the Netherlands in the 20th century, it served as the foundation for a newer model called → *Holacracy*. Characteristics inherited by Holacracy include the → *circle* model, → *consent* based decision-making and the → *double linking* between circles.

Spiral Dynamics

A model for human development, based on the core idea that there are different levels of human consciousness, each involving different value systems, life styles and worldviews. And as humanity evolves further, new levels of consciousness are coming into reach. Spiral Dynamics claims that the value systems and lifestyles inherent to each level emerged as adaptations to the specific conditions and problems of the time. For organizations, each level also entails typical modes of collaborating in groups, ranging in sophistication from a tyranny of the strongest to networked and decentralized organizations.

Stakeholder

Every person or group that has a stake, meaning a strong interest, in something. In the context of a → *transformation*, a stakeholder means anyone who can help or harm it. That's why, in transformation projects, stakeholder management is usually aimed at involving the relevant stakeholders. The goal is to generally increase the chances that they will support the project. Good stakeholder management can involve, for example, ensuring that the stakeholders get all the information they need.

Storytelling

Storytelling as a term usually means using a story to communicate a message, to convince people of something, to spark enthusiasm for it and so forth. Some authors claim that storytelling is a particularly effective way of communicating because humans have evolved a specific capacity for passing on knowledge in the form of stories. Concerns have been raised by some that this natural predilection could be used to manipulate people and spread false information by telling them untrue stories in a very compelling way. As the spread of urban legends indicates, this fear may not be completely unfounded.

Strategy

Originally a military term, strategy in the context of organizations typically means devising a long-term plan to ensure the success of the organization. Often, what this entails is that → *goals* are formulated, → *priorities* defined, and they are woven into a convincing narrative through good → *storytelling*. In the context of → *New Work,* strategy continues to play an important role, though it often doesn't result in long-term plans anymore. Rather, it tends to happen in the form of setting → *OKRs* or by defining strategic → *heuristics*. So just formulating a well-defined → *purpose* is not enough. Though the purpose describes the organization's very long-term ideal goal, it doesn't provide more short-term goals, focus areas or concrete projects. Without the necessary strategy work to do so, there's a danger that the organization's energy will dissipate and diminish through short-term misalignments.

Sync meeting

Similar to the tactical meeting in → *Holacracy*, the sync meeting is an operational meeting aimed at quick and effective synchronization of work between people. Hence the name. In the sync meeting, information is exchanged, next actions defined and all tensions resolved that are currently obstacles in the operational space of work. The goal is to be fast and deliver non-perfect outcomes, safe in the knowledge that all the topics covered in the meeting can be given more attention afterwards. Typically, this meeting is facilitated by a → *facilitator* role.

Teal

In his book → *Reinventing Organizations,* author Frederic Laloux describes different stages of organizational development, with the most sophisticated one called teal. Organizations at this stage have three key characteristics that set them apart: wholeness, self-organization, and evolutionary purpose.

Team

A team is any group of two or more people who have a shared goal and are motivated to organize themselves so as to achieve it. On one hand, a team comprises roles, allowing the total responsibility to be divided up. On the other hand, a team is composed of → *people* who have complex relationships with each other. These are dealt with in the → *tribe space.*

Tension

In the context of organizations, a tension is any unused potential. All → *people* always carry countless tensions in them in the form of, for example, ideas, questions and emotions. All these tensions can be used to fuel change and growth. This happens by translating them via → *proactive* thinking into small improvements. We recommend that you always view tensions as something positive, something that can be captured and harnessed for effecting meaningful change.

Transformation

In general, a transformation occurs when something changes its appearance or character. In the context of organizations, what we mean by a transformation is a significant change that happens in a person, a team, or at the level of the whole organization.

Tribe space

The space in which the relationships between people reside and can be examined. This can happen, for example, by installing a → *meeting* routine such as the → *Clear The Air* meeting. See → *Four Spaces.*

Win-Win Solution

A win-win solution has been found when the resolution of an issue creates no losers, only winners. To find such a solution, all participants must be willing to abandon their fixed opinions and seek alternative solutions. Looking for win-win solutions is often mentioned as a component of the paradigm shift from stiff hierarchical organizations to the more decentralized, less → *ego-driven* organizations of the future.

Work

In the world of organizations, we can define work as the cluster of all the activities that are undertaken to pursue the organization's purpose. Authors in the → *New Work* scene generally suggest that work should probably be redefined for the 21st century, because the current definition stems from the early 20th century, and new generations of workers are already questioning the notion of work as well as its value. Considering that most people spend most of their lives working, it seems reasonable to reflect on why and how we work.